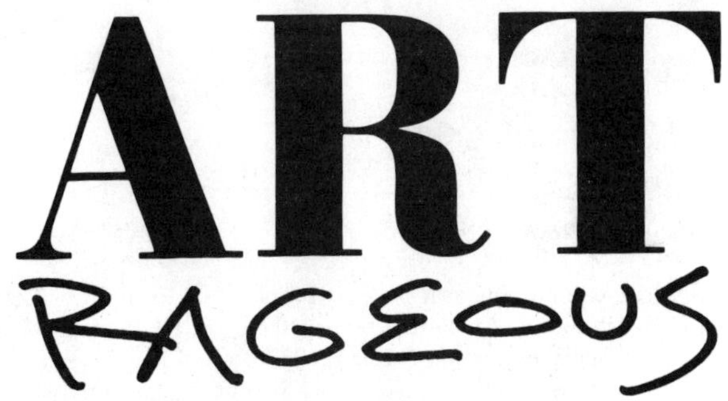


*Seminar notes and essays from Cornerstone Festival 1991*

**Colin Harbinson**
**Steve Scott**
**Rupert Loydell**
**Rick & Brenda Beerhorst**

CORNERSTONE PRESS
Chicago

Cornerstone Press is the publishing arm of Jesus People USA Evangelical Covenant Church, which is a community of believers serving the poor, the homeless and the elderly in the Uptown neighborhood of Chicago. If you would like more information about the community and its various oureaches, write JPUSA, c/o Cornerstone Press, 939 W. Wilson Ave. Ste. 202C, Chicago, IL 60640.



*Book design: Bruce Bitmead*
*Cover illustration: "Leaving the Corner II" 1990 by Rupert Loydell*

ISBN 0-940895-02-01
Printed in the United States of America.
99 98 97 96 95 94 93 92
8 7 6 5 4 3 2 1

Library of Congress Cataloging in Publication Data

# ART
RAGEOUS

# PREFACE

Christians and the arts haven't always mixed (and often still don't), so it is always good to see a publication like this happening. There *are* good Christian books about the arts, but many are heavyweight theology books, and I welcome another addition to the more readable and general end of the Christian market. I hope the writers in here will convince you, the reader, that the arts *do* matter and can be a part of Christian life. I personally haven't always found the mix easy to practice—there are many false idols along the way of any aspiring artist and writer!—but God gives strength to those genuinely searching and seeking His will.

These essays were initially given as lectures at Cornerstone Festival in 1991, an event that I was honoured to participate in. There I met others who, like me, are involved in not only *being* an artist, but *thinking the whole thing through;* people who are placing art within our twentieth-century Western culture, yet clearly drawing on their Christian faith. They may—like Steve Scott—turn to other cultures for inspiration and ideas, ways to make art appropriate to community needs. They may, like myself, need to clarify and reject many of the false claims of "spirituality" that modern fine-art critics make, or seek links across different arts disciplines in order to better understand how, and why, the arts function. All the authors seek to hold fast to the truth, but also journey into the fulfilling and rewarding world of emotion, craft, and delight that is the arts; a world that God has seen fit to give us in His wonderful creation; a world that is given for healing, recreation, and fullness of life.

These are exploratory essays, written with both the desire to find a rightful place for the arts in our midst and a willingness to share the findings of personal study and thought. They should be read as such, and not as definitive texts. They are starting points for your own discussion, consideration, and prayer. I welcome any dialogue and feedback this book may produce—I'm sure all the writers involved would agree.

By sharing these thoughts we move closer to an understanding of the width and depth of Christian community. At Cornerstone, the arts are coupled with the challenge of radical communal living that Jesus People USA (who organize the festival) present to the Uptown neighborhood of Chicago: a wonderful example of living among those in need, along with direct witness through both speech and deed—including music groups, poetry writing, magazine production, and painting. At England's Greenbelt (a festival much like Cornerstone, yet run by a series of committees who often meet only for this purpose), where I am involved in organizing the fine art exhibitions and seminars, the emphasis is on professionalism and celebration in the arts, coupled with the aim of raising political and social issues in a Christian context. Like Cornerstone, thousands of people come together to listen, share, praise, pray, sing, dance, talk, and learn.

There are many other similar festivals as well as churches, ad hoc groups, and individuals around the world engaged in similar exploration, discussion, and action. Many are alone, even within Christian communities. I hope that this book will be part of a move towards a holistic redemption where Christ is seen to be a force throughout all areas of our lives, an enabling and accompanying Saviour in the world of the arts, a catalyst in the Church of today, one who will heal division and misunderstanding.

RUPERT LOYDELL

# Acknowledgements

Colin Harbinson's essays originally appeared in the CANews © 1990 Colin Harbinson. Used by permission.

Steve Scott's work © 1991 Steve Scott. Used by permission.

Rupert Loydell's work © 1991 Rupert M. Loydell. His poems are from the collection *Fill These Days,* © 1990 Rupert M. Loydell, published by Stride, UK. Used by permission.

Rick and Brenda Beerhorst's work © 1991 Rick and Brenda Beerhorst. Used by permission.

This book would never have seen the light of day without the perseverance of Bruce Bitmead, who organized the material, designed and laid out the book, and acted as liaison between the authors and the publisher. Leah Grover, Sally Watkins, Nanci Fahey and Corey Fitz all worked on text entry; Sally and Kathryn Frank made the old Compugraphic typesetter sing, bringing all the galleys of type into existence. Special thanks to Jennifer Mullen who did a wonderful job as proofreader and line editor; her sharp eye brought the whole book into focus. A final thanks to Dawn Herrin and Pat Peterson; their commitment to book publishing is bearing fruit at last.

# Table of Contents

# 1

# The Arts: A Biblical Framework

*by*
*Colin Harbinson*

**COLIN HARBINSON is author and creator of *Toymaker and Son*, an award-winning allegory of the gospel that has been performed in over fifty countries. He is director of Youth With A Mission Academy of Performing Arts in Ontario, Canada.**

# Art and Revelation

The issue is hotly debated by Christians involved in the arts. There are strong feelings on both sides. The question in point is whether the arts are for "expression" or "communication." Those who want to communicate truth through the arts are accused of using art to produce a religious tract. They are accused of prostituting art in order to moralize. On the other hand, the Christian who does not use his artistic gift in the cause of the gospel is often perceived as having little commitment to Christ and certainly no heart for the lost. Creative expression that does not contain crucifixions, make overt references to the Trinity, or portray the whole Gospel is often seen as being of no value, and at worst, akin to serious backsliding.

As human beings we have a tendency to move toward extremes. Truth, however, is always held in tension. When it comes to art as expression or communication, it is not either/or, it's both. Each has its place, and if we fail to recognize that fact, we will not only be impoverished artistically and spiritually, but will end up misunderstanding and rejecting each other.

The purpose of this article is not to examine the merits of both positions outlined above. I do, however, want to explore art as communication, for the reason that a growing number of Christians are involved in creative expression within the sphere of proclamation. Furthermore, many of these overt gospel-bearing expressions demonstrate little understanding of either the place of art in the proclamative process, or what effective communication of truth should look like.

It is important to establish the fact that God communicates by way of revelation. Christianity is a revealed faith. The scriptural understanding of revelation is an "uncovering" or "showing." The content of revelation is the uncovering and showing of truth. For the artist, this should come as both an encouragement and a challenge. Art works best when it "shows" rather than "tells." Art is at its best when it uncovers what familiarity has concealed, and opens up to a fresh perspective of truth; the truth about any subject. This would strongly suggest that artistic expression, at its best, is compatible with God's way of revealing truth to man. Both show and both seek to show truth.

The nineteenth chapter of Psalms (verses 1 & 2) declares that "the heavens are *telling* of the glory of God; and their expanse is *declaring* the work of His hands. Day to day *pours forth speech,* and night to night *reveals knowledge.*" God's creative expression is proclamative; it tells, declares and pours forth speech. It does this by way of revelation; it "reveals knowledge."

Jesus was the ultimate revelation; "the word made flesh." He alone could say, "He who has seen me has seen the Father." Incarnational reality is essential understanding for the artist. Art has to do with "fleshing out" truth from ideas, thoughts, and concepts.

When Jesus communicated, it was out of the deeply rooted understanding that if man was to be truly changed, it would be as a result of receiving and acting on revelation granted by the Father. The thirteenth chapter of Matthew records an enlightening response that Jesus gave when His disciples asked Him why He spoke in parables. He said, "To you it has been granted to know the mysteries of the kingdom of heaven, but to them it has not been granted. . . . Therefore I speak to them in parables; because while seeing they do not see, and while hearing they do not hear, nor do they understand."

On the surface, this would appear to be a strange theory of communication. Those who asked Jesus the way to eternal life were told stories! If that wasn't enough, His stories often left them more confused! Why did the Great Communicator not make things crystal clear? His response to their questions seemed to provoke more questions. Jesus often ended His stories with the phrase, "He who has ears, let him hear." He was obviously concerned with something much more important than the simple passing of information. He wanted transformation through revelation. Transformation was possible when people heard with their spiritual ears. In his book, *The Unfolding Kingdom*, Lawson writes, "The parables are not made deliberately difficult. But for those who do not wish to commit themselves to their inner message, all they will hear are stories, pure and simple."

Jesus wanted people to search for the pearl of great price, so that when they found it, they would sell everything they had in order to obtain it.

Our creative communication should be of such a nature that it requires something of its audience—asking questions—and allowing God to grant revelation to those who have ears to hear. The temptation to overcommunicate in order that everyone will understand everything is a misguided notion. We must resist the tendency to give neatly packaged answers; it is not the Jesus style.

An example of powerful and effective communication is recorded in the second book of Samuel, when King David is confronted by the prophet Nathan. David was a man after God's own heart, yet we find him on an escalating pathway of deliberate and wrong moral choices. He sent for Bathsheba, knowing that she was Uriah's wife, and slept with her. He unsuccessfully tried to cover her resulting pregnancy. David finally sent a message that ensured Uriah's death. After Bathsheba's husband was killed, David took her to be his wife.

Nathan had a formidable challenge before him when he went to confront David. He was facing a king who had taken every precaution to cover up his sin, and for all intents and purposes save God's, had succeeded. How could Nathan persuade this man, who had shown so little compassion, of the gravity of his sin in the sight of God? He told David a story and told him to judge it!

Simply put, Nathan told of two men; one rich, the other poor. The rich man had plenty of sheep, but the poor man had nothing save for a little lamb. When a traveler came to the home of the rich man, no animal was taken from among his flocks; rather, he went down to the poor man's house and took his one lamb, killed it, and served it up for the guest to eat.

David was enraged at this story and immediately pronounced judgement. He said, "That man had no compassion! He ought to die!" You can almost feel the electricity of that moment, when Nathan looked King David in the face and declared, "You are that man!" It was a moment of profound revelation that caused the deep repentance of David found in the fifty-first psalm.

Nathan's communication was effective, but not by accident. By isolating four of the elements in this incident, we will find principles that are important in the context of our present discussion.

Firstly, *the communicator was not isolated*. Nathan lived in the middle of the action. He knew what was going on. As artists we must not retreat to a cozy, safe Christian subculture and expect to create works that relate to the culture at large. Jesus told stories in response to what people were doing and saying. His parables were never in a vacuum. We are called to walk in the middle of our culture, asking God for grace and cleansing.

Secondly, *the communication was relevant*. It was not a coincidence that Nathan used a lamb in his story. David the shepherd-boy-turned-king found a deep, resonating note within himself and became instantly involved. Nathan, using the power of story line, drew deep emotional responses from David. Our art must explore universal truths that are commonly shared in the language of our cultural experience and expression.

Thirdly, *the communication was not "preachy."* The story that Nathan told "uncovered" the truth that David had concealed. David had no idea the story was about himself. His barriers were down, and the Holy Spirit was able to "show" him his sinful heart in a moment of revelation. The story did not preach or moralize, but gave David an opportunity to "look in" and make an objective judgement.

Lastly, *the communication was creative*. Nathan did not tell the same story—once upon a time a king walked on the roof of his palace and saw a beautiful . . . !! Art is not a photocopy of reality. Art by definition is indirectional. Picasso observed that "art is a lie that tells the truth." It is a lens through which reality can be perceived and revelation received.

In conclusion, art is at its best when it uncovers what familiarity has concealed. It is making the familiar, unfamiliar, so that it can be revisited with fresh eyes. It allows for objective judgement as artist and audience meet at the point of the work of art. It is a shared experience. No room here for preaching or moralizing, but rather a powerful place of potential revelation as truth is "uncovered" and "shown."

# The Arts and Spiritual Warfare

Spiritual warfare is a subject of great interest and discussion among Christians today. Some would have us believe that because Jesus defeated Satan at Calvary, we need no longer concern ourselves with spiritual warfare—Jesus did it all! Others act as though they believe that the Cross had little or no effect on the powers of darkness, and that it has been largely left to us to defeat Satan!

As always, truth is held in tension. Our understanding of spiritual warfare in the life of the believer must be firmly rooted in our understanding of the definitive victory that Jesus has already won. Anything less is to totally misunderstand the finished work of the Cross. However, Scripture is very clear in the mandate it gives to us as we walk out our faith. We too can have daily victory over the power of the enemy in our lives. He only has the authority that we give him. Our faith is not to be passive or defensive. We are to pull down strongholds with the spiritual weapons at our disposal. The victory of Calvary enables us to defeat the enemy, for without the Cross we would be at Satan's mercy.

A hallmark of truth is its universal application. We can perceive truth in a particular theological or practical framework and fail to make the "connection" with other areas of reality. Like Elisha's servant, we need to have our eyes opened to see beyond physical observation to spiritual reality and practical application (2 Kings 6:17, 18).

Nowhere is the truth of spiritual warfare more needed or so little understood as in the area of the arts. This sad fact has left artists open to the attacks of the enemy, resulting in many unnecessary casualties. As artists we struggle with very specific issues in our lives, yet often fail to realize that ''our struggle is not against flesh and blood, but against the rulers, against the powers, against the world forces of this darkness, against the spiritual forces of wickedness in the heavenly places'' (Eph. 6:12).

In over twenty-five years of involvement in the arts, the most vital understanding I have gained is of the nature and significance of spiritual warfare as it relates to the arts and the artist. A number of years ago the leadership of the Academy of Performing Arts received a very powerful vision from the Lord which has undergirded and guided all that we have been involved in ever since. We saw a picture of fortified cities on which were written the names of various art forms. Over each city there were principalities and powers, among which were idolatry, pride, independence, and impurity. We believe the Lord spoke to us that the arts were His good gifts to be expressed for beauty and glory. We were to pull down these strongholds and see the arts reconciled to God. With this mandate came a warning. We were to make sure the strongholds over the arts were not strongholds of the enemy in our own lives. If we did not experience personal victory over idolatry, pride, independence, and impurity, we would not only fail to bring reconciliation, but would ourselves be drawn into these same areas. Many a person has entered into the arts with a heart to glorify God through their expression and gifting, and very quickly found themselves far away from Him. If we want to be ''salt and light'' in the culture, we must first allow the ''salt'' of God to cleanse us, and let His ''light'' shine in us exposing our own darkness. Unresolved areas of our lives give the enemy a foothold and platform from which to launch his fiery darts. There are many artists who are spiritual casualties because they did not allow God first of all to deal with these specific issues in their own lives.

I would like to suggest four practical and proven ways that will help us as artists to effectively walk in victory. We need to know how to discern spiritual strongholds, understand the nature of spiritual authority, walk in the opposite spirit, and build our own spiritual citadel.

*The discerning of spiritual strongholds* is of primary importance. Different locations, cities, and nations have their own specific spiritual oppression. As our performing troupes have traveled internationally, they have found themselves facing specific struggles in certain locations. That is the nature of operation of ''spiritual forces of wickedness in the heavenly places''! In one city they will face attacks in the area of impurity; in another situation they'll find themselves rising up in pride and arrogance. Instead of passive sightseeing in new locales, we need to walk in the streets in active intercession, asking God to show us the principalities and powers over a city or nation. As God shows us, we can take our authority in the Lord. Biblical battles were won in the spiritual realm before they were won in the natural. Knowing where the enemy will attack, we can prepare ourselves for defensive and offensive action. This principle also applies to theaters and performance areas. If Shinto priests are flown in from Japan to Broadway prior to the opening of a show in order to cleanse the theater of "negative" influences, how much more do we need to be aware of this principle in the realm of our spiritual warfare as artists.

Secondly, we need to understand *the nature of our spiritual authority*. Victory is not assured by just resisting the enemy. Many try to resist but get nowhere! The reason for failure is that we ignore the full counsel of Scripture. Resisting is proceeded by submitting. "Submit therefore to God. Resist the devil and he will flee from you" (James 4:7). If our lives are not submitted to God, we have no authority whatsoever. We have no power at all. Authority comes out of submission. This principle applies to the God-given accountability structure in our lives. I am not referring to ungodly control, but to godly accountability. As artists, our biggest need is to be spiritually discipled by those who love us enough to speak into our lives. We need relationships where we can be open about our struggles and receive prayer and encouragement in the Lord.

A third principle is that of *walking in the opposite spirit:* "A gentle answer turns away wrath" (Prov. 15:1). Idolatry is a major stronghold in the arts. Art has the ability to draw away our love for the Lord and focus our affection on itself. The opposite of idolatry is worship of God. Artists must first of all be worshippers. That sets our focus. If we worship the Lord in spirit and truth, art will never become an idol. Worship must be a "lifestyle" for us. Humility is the opposite of pride. Humility in our lives and our art. As Franky Schaeffer says in his book *Sham Pearls for Real Swine*, "Humility is a vigorous state of being in which we have a sense of who we are, and more importantly, who we are not."

We come against independence by embracing dependence on God and the Body of Christ. Even though we are misunderstood and criticized by some, we can not walk in independence and separation from other believers. Independence is the doorway to deception. We cannot be God's agents of reconciliation in the arts and be unreconciled to His Church. We must find a spiritual home where we can give as well as receive from our brothers and sisters in the Lord.

Finally, we are to walk in purity and righteousness, which is the opposite of impurity. In an area where sensuality abounds, we must allow God to deal with roots of impurity in our lives so that we can present our bodies as a living sacrifice, holy, acceptable to Him (Rom. 12:1).

Walking in the opposite spirit to strongholds in the arts both defines our lifestyles and releases spiritual authority. As artists, we need to have a lifestyle of worship, walking in humility and dependence, having "presented our members as instruments of righteousness" (Rom. 6:13).

The fourth principle involves the *building of a citadel in our lives*. In the Old Testament, a citadel was a fortress built in the center of the city in an elevated place. It contained food and weapons in case the enemy breached the outer wall of the city. From a citadel the citizens could withstand a siege and continue to fight the enemy. As artists, we must have that place in our own lives where we can go for spiritual food—a place where we can do spiritual warfare against the attack of the enemy. It is too late to build a citadel in the heat of battle; it must be built in peace time. One of the great tragedies is that people involve themselves in the arts without building a citadel, without having a solid and growing relationship with the Lord. The result is spiritual genocide.

If I have been strong in the statements I have made, it is only because I love the arts and desire that as artists we truly glorify God in the expression of our gifts. The charge of Scripture to "walk in a manner worthy of [our] calling" (Eph. 4:1) must ring loudly in our ears. We need not wallow in our struggles and use the excuse that we walk a difficult path. We are open to specific attacks and temptations, but we do not have to succumb. As artists we are not just called to maintain the status quo; we are called to a much higher task. As we pursue our gifts and calling in God, we will be agents of reconciliation in the arts. As we face the reality of spiritual warfare, we must remind ourselves that the "weapons of our warfare are not of the flesh, but divinely powerful for the destruction of fortresses [strongholds]" (2 Cor. 10:4).

# The Test of Humility

The responses range from embarrassed blushes to mutual admiration. We find the "pretend I didn't hear" strategy, and the "it's really Jesus in me" attitude. Not to be forgotten is the spectacle of hands raised heavenward in a display of public piety. We are, of course, referring to the different ways in which people respond to the praise or applause of others.

A major concern to us as artists is to get our work "out there." We want our creative work to be experienced and responded to. When met with acclaim and success we struggle with knowing what our response as Christians should be. The book of Proverbs (27:21) tells us that we are tested by our response to the praise of others. Honesty will cause us to admit that we often fail the test!

The "world" of the arts is a showcase for monumental egos. Narcissists and prima donnas roam freely, seeking to perpetuate the myth of the artist as a special creation. Self-absorption, combining itself with selfish ambition and self-promotion, creates a scenario which inevitably ends in self-destruction. Ignoring the fact that God will not give His glory to another (Isa. 42:8), many artists heap upon themselves the adulation and worship that is misdirected toward them. As Christians working in the arts, we must, in a very real sense, be "in the 'world,' but not of it."

Success and acclaim are not incompatible with a lifestyle of humility. In fact, as we shall see, when humility is embraced we can expect even greater recognition than we imagined! Artistic excellence, when combined with excellence of character, is an explosive dynamic.

Pride is a "self" problem which manifests itself in two major ways. In one we find **self-elevation** which demonstrates the overvaluing of oneself. This can be easily identified as pride, due to the attendant boasting and self-promotion. The second way is a **self-debasing** form of pride, although not usually identified as such. This is the "worm" syndrome that confuses humility with inferiority. Much of the struggle with pride comes, interestingly, from a foundation of insecurity, inferiority, and rejection.

The following branches of the root of pride are not exhaustive, but will serve to focus on and identify areas of common struggle.

**A Competitive Attitude:** I am not satisfied with the way God made me, and I find myself looking at others, envying their recognition, and wanting to be the one praised and elevated.

**Independence:** Reserving the right to do my own thing, I am a "free spirit" who will not submit to any authority.

**Reputation:** Believing in my self-importance, I expect to receive preferential treatment.

**A Critical Attitude:** Thinking myself better than others, I speak negatively and disloyally about them.

**Self-protection:** Because I have been wounded in my emotions, I refuse vulnerability by building a wall of protection around my life.

**Fear of failure:** I avoid new challenges and stay in the "comfort zone," because I want others to see me in a successful light.

**Arrogance and aggression:** I have an unteachable attitude and do not easily accept correction from others.

**False humility:** Having the pride of the "worm," I do not acknowledge my gifts, but put myself down so that others will praise me.

**Perfectionism:** Driving myself and others to meet impossible standards, I am unwilling to do, or associate with, anything that does not meet my perfectionist expectations.

A brief look at the life of King Uzziah (2 Chron. 26) will shed further light on the ability of pride and selfish ambition to rob us of our destiny in God. This young king grew, with God's help, into a great, creative leader. At the height of success and fame something tragic occurred:

> When he became *strong*, his heart was so proud that he acted corruptly, and he was unfaithful to the Lord his God (2 Chron. 26:16).

On the road to success the problem was hidden, but when fame and recognition were at their peak his true heart was revealed. Pride led him to believe that he could do what he wanted, even to the point of disobeying God's law. When confronted with his sin, he demonstrated an angry heart and an unteachable attitude. The immediate judgment of God caused King Uzziah to have leprosy for the rest of his days. On his death there was no state funeral or long public eulogy; they simply said, "He was a leper"!

What a tragic end to a life with so much potential.

God hates, abominates (Prov. 6:16, 17), and opposes (James 4:6) pride. We do well at this juncture to ponder for a moment the implications of the words of Jesus when He said, "Everyone who exalts himself shall be humbled" (Luke 14:11)

There is a different road that as Christians we are called to walk. It is a kingdom road where pride and selfish ambition give way to humility and servanthood, a road already marked by the footprints of Jesus, its signposts emblazoned with His words of encouragement that "he who humbles himself shall be exalted" (Luke 14:11).

Humility is knowing our real value. It is a willingness to be transparent and vulnerable about our weaknesses, as well as our strengths. Humility is a healthy condition, not a sickly attitude. We can be strong and confident in the giftings that God has given us while at the same time acknowledging our utter dependence upon Him and our need of each other.

The life of King Nebuchadnezzar is a redemptive story that illustrates the power of humility. This king became a legend in his own mind as he fantasized about his greatness. This state of unreality lead to a period of insanity, until he finally came to the place of acknowledging that "Now I Nebuchadnezzar praise, exalt, and honor the King of heaven, for . . . He is able to humble those who walk in pride" (Dan. 4:37). God not only forgave the king, but put him back on his throne and gave him greater authority and glory than before!

God could do that because He could now trust Nebuchadnezzar to give Him the glory in any situation. Pride is destructive in our lives, but true humility is a powerful spiritual weapon and a key to "surpassing glory." There is no limit to what God can give a person who truly walks in humility.

God loves humility and requires that we walk in it (Mic. 6:8). He wants to see stubborn hearts broken of their self-willfulness (Isa. 66:2). Pride must be confessed as sin and hated, abominated, and opposed wherever we find it in our lives. Humility is a do-it-yourself process! We are to clothe *ourselves* in humility (1 Pet. 5:5). Making a moment-by-moment choice to walk in openness before God and each other. Humility is not an instant state of being, the answer to a few fervent prayers. We begin the journey by making a conscious choice to *"set our hearts"* on walking in humility, making it a special desire and focus of our life (Dan. 10:12).

We can be confident in the artistic gifts that God has given us. When recognition and acclaim come our way, we do not need to walk in false humility under the guise of personal piety. Gracious acceptance and acknowledgement are appropriate responses to the gifts of praise and affirmation. We hold them lightly in our hands as we offer our thanks and appreciation to the Giver, while in our hearts we say, "Thank you, Lord. I appreciate you!"

# 2

# Scratching the Surface

*by*
*Steve Scott*

**STEVE SCOTT is a singer, songwriter and musician, poet and multimedia artist. His involvement in the arts takes him across the U.S. and overseas, including recent trips to Indonesia, Russia, and England. He lives in Sacramento, California, with his wife and two daughters.**

# Lost Steps / Drawing Conclusions

> No human choreography can equal the eurhythmy of a branch outlined against the sky. I asked myself whether the higher forms of the aesthetic emotion do not consist merely in a supreme understanding of creation. A day will come when men will discover an alphabet in the eyes of chalcedonies, in the markings of the moth, and will learn in astonishment that every spotted snail has always been a poem.
>
> —Alejo Carpentier, *The Lost Steps*

In his novel Alejo Carpentier tells the story of an ethnomusicologist who goes off on an expedition into the South American jungle in search of primitive musical instruments. The story tells us about the discoveries the character makes as he goes deeper and deeper into the jungle, both about the primitive origins of music and about himself. At last, he spends some time living with a tribe deep in the jungle and feels that he is perhaps reborn, discovering his "true" self among members of this community.

He decides to live the rest of his life with them, but first he realizes that he must travel back to the "outside world" and settle a few affairs. He travels back along a river, carefully marking trees along the bank in order to find his way back into the jungle once his business is complete. While he is in the outside world there is a tremendous downpour of rain that causes the river to rise, and in some cases overflow its banks. When he attempts to go back into the jungle along the way that he came, he finds that the changed water level of the river has obscured the carefully marked trail. Hence the title *The Lost Steps*.

In the passage from the book quoted above, the author suggests that our sense of beauty, creativity, and the aesthetic is in fact nothing more than a dim, muffled echo of an original perception of the wonders of the natural world around us. He seems to be suggesting that we, too, have journeyed away from that primary recognition of our ''selves'' and the beauty of the created order, and that the idea of a journey back is as hopeless a quest as that of the ethnomusicologist seeking to return to his ''true self'' somewhere in the heart of the jungle. The trail has vanished. The steps are lost. Given that the author intends the story of his ethnomusicologist to be a metaphor for some aspect of our human condition, I'd like to turn attention briefly to metaphor itself.

In the course of these remarks, we are going to use certain metaphors to either help us travel from one level of meaning to another or to draw fresh meanings from the comparison of previously unconnected images. In the first kind of metaphor, we proceed from that which is known and make it a basis of comparison with the unknown. When we talk about ''the milk of human kindness,'' for example, we move from something we are familiar with (milk) to a more abstract concept (kindness). We could call this kind of metaphor an ''escalator metaphor'' because it carries us from familiar ground up to something new. Then there is the other kind of metaphor I am going to refer to from time to time, which brings together two previously unconnected images or subjects and allows us to grasp a new meaning in the light of their juxtaposition. It works a little like those viewfinder toys that combines two images into one with added three-dimensional depth.

Now, I'm saying this because I believe metaphor to be central to the way we think about art, and also the way we think about spirituality. I hope we can find some way of building a bridge between the two.

For this first talk I am trying to give a general overview of just a few of my ideas about art, and in order to proceed I want to refer back to my early memories of art school. One of the things we used to do was draw—and I mean *draw*—a composed still life or a human figure over the period of several hours, sometimes filling an entire day. In the event of an arranged still life of inanimate objects, the drawing exercise could stop and be resumed the next day. The idea was not so much to arrive at a ''finished drawing'' in the conventional sense, but to get involved in the process of observation, learning how to record what we saw and correct what we recorded. When we think about drawing in this way I believe we can come up with a couple of useful observations.

Firstly, by the time our still life—or whatever—had been reproduced on paper, it had changed scale, color, and had become, if you like, a *field* of juxtaposed shapes on flat paper. It involved, necessarily, a reduction in scale, a collapsing from three dimensions to two, and a substitution of monochrome for color. It was, therefore, already a radical abstraction, and as such the drawer in the very act of making marks either recorded or created a flat plane of visual relationships.

Also, the process of making such a drawing involved an ongoing self-correcting process. The process went through an entire cycle from initial observation to mark on paper. It could almost be described as a loop. The eye observed. The mind processed the information and informed the muscles in the shoulder and the arm, which in turn directed the hand guiding the pencil across the paper. Look at the mark, look at the object, correct the mark in the light of renewed perception.

So here we have two "images" derived from the act/process of drawing. What is being produced in one way (going back to our first image) is a flat "field" of information in which the objects and the spaces surrounding them are reduced to abstract shapes; all of them, for the purpose of the drawing, related one to another. When we look at this act/process of drawing in the light of our second image, the "cycle/loop" metaphor, what we have is an inclusive self-maintaining system, a self-correcting, interrelated "ecology" of observation and mark making that sustains the process of drawing. And of course, I am using "ecology" metaphorically, too. The word is more at home in the realm of the various interacting life systems in the natural environment than in a life drawing class.

I want to move from this "ecology" of drawing, this self- maintaining loop of observation and correction, to the larger ecology of God's created world as the Bible talks about it.

The Apostle Paul wrote to the Romans concerning God's order, wisdom, and power made visible through the creation. You do not have to go too far in the New Testament to find other references to the orderliness of God's creation, or its relationship to us. The systems and patterns of organization in the natural animal and plant world are alluded to throughout the entire Bible as evidence of God's orderly creativity and moral and ethical concerns. According to Paul's letter to the Colossians, the work of Christ included both the creation and the redemption of all things in heaven and on earth . . . the material universe.

Not only is the visible creation in some way a reflection of the invisible, but personal, God and, in fact, currently kept going "sustained" by the power of His word, but it is also something purified and "reconciled" by the work of Christ on the cross. The significance of this larger dimension of the cross has not been lost on some Christian thinkers. For instance, the writer Wesley Granberg Michaelson, in his book *A Worldly Spirituality,* uses close analysis of biblical texts combined with extensive quotation from a wide range of Christian writers, ancient and modern, to point out that there is not only a "personal" and "cosmic" dimension to the work of the cross, but there is also an ecological dimension. This should impact our reading of the biblical guidelines for stewardship and discipleship.

Other thinkers coming from different philosophical viewpoints have tried to widen and deepen our understanding and appreciation of the vast, interactive, interdependent system that we know as "the natural world." Theorists such as Gregory Bateson have argued for a larger, more inclusive "grasp" on the complexity of the natural world and our relationship to it.

He and others have talked in terms of complex interacting systems of information present at *all* levels of reality but acutely observable in the natural world. Some theorists see patterns of organization in nature, and even some patterns of organization in culture, to be participating elements in a larger, interactive "whole" of which we, the observers, are only a part. And, of course, this interactive, "holistic" approach to understanding the interrelated systems of nature, culture and life hinges upon the recognition that we are inside and *part* of the very system we are trying to analyze and observe. Ideas like these challenge older ideas of detached, "objective" observation—and the insistence on the neutrality and purity of those observation methods. Ideas like these also call into question those neatly defined categories of "value" and "fact."

Slowly we have come, in a variety of fields from physics to linguistics, to recognize the limitations of our methods of analysis and our metaphors. As we reach out for more organic, inclusive ways of describing how things work and relate to one another, we also keep in mind that (to use Michael Polanyi's phrase) knowledge is "personal." Also, the very language we use to try and describe this "personal knowledge" is not without its built-in agendas and presuppositions, either.

If what we are talking about is a large, self-sustaining system that finds reflections and echoes in other parts of the creation, from nature to culture, and perhaps even concept and language; then we might well ask what invisible attributes of God were reflected and represented in and by the visible created order, according to Paul's line of thinking. The wisdom, creativity, and morality of God, certainly. But surely there is more. Is there a primary level of reality, involving an invisible yet personal God, that the self-sustaining and interactive system of the natural, visible order was/is intended to point us back to? I believe there is.

When we think of councils, creeds, and early church fathers we tend to think of the drive towards the clarification of central doctrines. We think of the Incarnation, the Virgin Birth, etc. One such set of ideas, argued about vigorously then and, in some circles, now, was the idea of the Trinity. The Bible doesn't mention the Trinity as a conceptual unit. It just narrates what happens as the members of the triune Godhead work together. The biblical materials focus mainly on demonstrating the interactive participation of each member of the triune Godhead in the sustaining, redeeming, and transforming of the created realm.

In the Gospels, the Father honors the Son, the Son sends the Spirit, the Spirit draws to the Son, the Son says, "If you've seen me, you've seen the Father"—each member of the Godhead maintaining individual identity in the very act of conferring honor and support upon another member. And also allowing metaphoric relationship to occur. Jesus healed on the Sabbath and used the metaphor of a child playing in his Father's workshop (John 5). The Pharisees were invited to compare two classes of activity and concern.

God the Father cares for creation. So do I. I simply act in imitation of what I have seen, says Jesus in defense of His claim to Sonship. In another part of John's Gospel Jesus replies to Philip's request to see God the Father. "If you've seen me, you've seen the father." Jesus was suggesting that the Father's character was revealed in the details of the earthly life of Jesus. For a disciple, a close companion of Jesus, the opportunity was there to build from the known (Jesus's life observed) to the unknown (the nature of the Father). Would this qualify as an "escalator" metaphor?

Paul wrote to the Philippians that Jesus demonstrated precisely who He is by the very act of letting go of the privilege of equality with God.

It should not seem strange to speak (even if metaphorically) of an *ecology* of the triune Godhead. Nor should it seem strange to suggest, in line with what Paul tells the Romans, that the visible ecological system was intended to provide a working analogy for the "primary ecology" of the Godhead. Could this be another of our "escalator" metaphors?

Henry Drummond, a scientific writer at the close of the last century, wrote a book called 'Natural Law in the Spiritual World' in which he explored the relationships, analogies, whatever between the world of nature and the spiritual realm. His thesis was that analogies and comparisons could be drawn between the two realms because they both shared the same operating dynamic, the same set of rules. What if one of the rules linking them was that of interactive, participatory servanthood such as we see in the various interrelated life systems? such as we see in the Trinity?

Now at this point (and what I mean by "this point" is our original reference to what Paul said early in Romans about the intention behind the created order) things start to get a bit dark, because Paul goes on to talk about people "exchanging the truth for a lie" and suppressing within themselves the knowledge of God. He goes on in Romans 8 to talk about creation being "subject to futility." Or, to go back to our opening remarks, the "steps being lost."

I want to suggest that part of the knowledge that Paul talks about being crushed is this awareness of the bridge between the two "ecologies," the contingent ecology of the created realm and the primary ecology of the triune Godhead. Once that information goes astray or gets distorted, then there are all sorts of implications for how we think about *nature* (and we have had models of the world that go from the very mechanical to the very "organic" hypothesizing one giant living entity), how we think about our *selves* in relation to nature (who are we—captains of our fate, or just a bundle of chemicals in a bag of skin?) or even how we think about *how we think* (should we rely on logic and pure reason, or should we build conclusions simply on the evidence of our senses? Or do we, in fact, create the world as we see it? Is the imagination primary? Are the poets the "unacknowledged legislators?") And of course all those secondary corruptions and distortions make their way into how we think and behave as a society, and affect how we evaluate right, wrong, good, bad, progress, weakness, power, etc. And these corruptions turn up in our creativity.

The fact that we *create* carries echoes of the truth that we are created beings reliant upon the grace of a creative God. However, *what* we create very often bears the hallmarks of our fallen nature.

In order to carry on our exploration of some of the ideas that are arising from these remarks, I am going to talk briefly about art and the way in which it functions in two cultures. I believe the contrasting functions of art will bear out the implications of some of the things already said, and also carry them further.

The arts have taken different directions in different cultures. In the West we can look back over a long line of development in the area of the arts, going back to artistic expression rooted variously in "classical" virtues in which Greek ideas of beauty and truth were channeled through art. As the worldviews changed, so did the role of the arts, and many artists began to use their skills in the service of Christendom, and then more in accurate analytical rendition of the observable world. This moved on to an attempt to accurately render the business of perception itself. This, in turn, gave way to a quest for inner truth that found symbolic outer expression, ranging from dream imagery through to various degrees of abstraction. More recently, artists began to work purely and simply in terms of relationships of color, scale, tone, and texture. They exploited the acutely material characteristics and properties of their chosen medium. Now, I personally believe that abstract art "works" when you look at it, because in terms of its internal relationships it carries a distant echo—at least in the seeing heart of the observer—of the Primary Reality which, we know from the analogous springboard of nature, is one of mutual cooperation and dynamic interdependence. As Ecclesiastes put it, "He has made everything beautiful in its time. He has also set eternity in the hearts of men; yet they cannot fathom what God has done from beginning to end" (Eccles. 3:11).

Where such work becomes "subject to futility" along with the rest of the created order, in my opinion, is when it "argues" its existence in purely "formal" terms, denying all prior reference. It has, if you like, a "form of Godliness, but denies the power thereof." Sometimes it becomes a platform for the mythical genius and godlike "sensitivity" of the artist, and all the attendant intellectual and cultural snobbery that goes with that fiction. So either the *artwork* or the *artist* claims some mystical privileged realm, denying the very primary reality its organization of shapes and textures bears traces of, or denying the source of creativity and inspiration that gifts the artist.

In a culture like the Balinese one we have a reversal of the equation. There is no separate word or concept for "art" as we understand it. Art, everyday life, and spirituality are delicately interwoven. Everyone participates, making rice and flower offerings, participating in or observing ceremonial dances, dramas, and shadowplays. The Balinese blend a native animism with Hinduism and come up with a worldview in which every aspect of the world has a spiritual and magical meaning. The conventional categories, "sacred" and "secular," are meaningless, because there is a subtle interpenetration of the spiritual and material in all walks of life. The religious quest, therefore, is one of finding harmonic balance, maintaining equilibrium between the natural and supernatural elements. And the artistic quest, accordingly, is to symbolically express this searching *for* and finding *of* balance. In some cases that equilibrium is sought in the dramatic reenactment of traditional stories or the drama of powerful conflict. In other cases that equilibrium is searched for not in mere reenactment, but in going into trance and being taken over by the forces in question. All in all, the search is for balance in spirituality, life, and artistic expression. The quest for beauty and harmony in the arts, therefore, is considered a sacred spiritual task.

So, in summary, the role of the arts is central to maintaining a "beautiful" balance of those three interwoven categories.

While a culture like Bali is healthy, in my opinion, in its recognition of spiritual values in art, and also the context of art in everyday life, it "subjects the created order to futility" by virtually deifying this created order through its animistic/Hindu belief system. So instead of an autonomous, self-defining art object such as in recent Western History, we have a worship of the created order. *Both* cultures carry echoes of the Primary Truth in the fact that they make something we identify as art. *Both* cultures display the fallen nature of their participants, as I have suggested, in culturally particular ways.

We have traveled a long way from the drawing classes I took over twenty years ago and also from our opening quote from—and remarks about—Alejo Carpentier's novel *The Lost Steps*. We have traveled from the "system" of observation and mark making to the system of nature. We went from there to the interactive servant characteristics of the Trinity itself, and then we took a lead from the Apostle Paul's line of thinking in the book of Romans to see how suppression of ''the true knowledge of God'' might start to manifest itself in the art forms of different cultures.

In order to get us thinking in that direction we contrasted two cultures, one that virtually made an absolute of the art form and one that made a god of the natural environment. All of these remarks and suggestions proceeded less in the form of a systematic lecture, and more in the form of a story that leapfrogged from image and metaphor to image and metaphor, somewhat along the lines of our opening descriptions of how some kinds of metaphor work. In short, we have been inside the very thing we have been trying to describe.

# ART AND PROPHETIC CONFRONTATION: THE ZEAL OF THINE HOUSE

We ended on a fairly lofty note in our previous remarks, and to begin our gradual descent down the mountain I want to pursue this trinitarian idea further. Firstly, I want to follow Dorothy Sayers' lead and map out three areas of the "art process" and assign them (provisionally, just for the sake of imagery, metaphor, and our discussion) to members of the Godhead. When we consider the various aspects of creation and redemption, these categories seem to work.

Secondly, I want to use a "threefold paradigm" to try and model the artistic "event," i.e., the object and its reception.

Thirdly, Later in the talk I hope to descend even further into the world of material and particulars and look at how three creative people in the Bible looked for creative ways of revealing the heart of God to man. I'm following an approach to Trinity and art first sketched out, I believe, by Dorothy Sayers.

When it comes to considering the use of the image of the triune Godhead as a model for understanding the "components" of the creative act, I believe it involves stepping back from the holistic, "interactive" model we touched on previously and considering each member of the Godhead individually.

## FATHER: FROM THE IDEA TO THE MATERIAL EXPRESSION

God speaks and it moves out of the realm of pure thought into created "reality," with dimensions of space and time plus location and materiality.

## SON: THE "TENSION" BETWEEN FORM AND CONTENT

Many of the classical problems surrounding the Incarnation and the classic attempts to explain it revolve around issues that resemble the concerns of the interaction between form and content in art.

Does art form contain a message (content?) or is the form somehow the message? Admittedly many of the questions, ancient and modern, about the Incarnation tell us more about the limitations of our world model and its constricting influence on our language (and of course vice versa). Similar questions surround art. What a picture is "about" for many people has more to do with drawn images than color values. We have touched on the futility of a modern art that sought purity by shrugging off all associations.

Art critics such as the late Peter Fuller had pointed out the messianic pretensions of some work like this, work that attempts to "incarnate" the essential nature of art (or this particular artist's vision or particular artwork) by the self- emptying gesture of the art object. Nonetheless, in spite of all of our brute misunderstandings and the mystical pretensions of others, the subtlety of the relationships between Christ's human and divine natures and art's form and content bear some family resemblances.

## SPIRIT: THE BUSINESS OF RECEPTION

The Holy Spirit stirs the imagination and the conscience, breaks the hard ground of our indifference, and seems to answer to that area of the artistic experience (or could we say any experience of communication, even those experiences that we deem a mystery) that involves reception and response. In the biblical language there is a quickening of the Spirit but also a quenching of it. This area of response and reception is not only brought into play as we recognize ourselves in the held-up mirror of some art, but it is also there in the faint echo in the heart's depths when we look upon other art.

This initial sweep through the trinitarian model out of the way, it only remains to comment further, briefly, on the phenomena of "response" and "reception" before we get down to those creative biblical characters who revealed aspects of God's heart towards His creation.

If we go back to our earlier model of "art" as self- sustaining system, I believe we can describe the art *experience* as a holistic totality rather than a series of hard components.

Art is not merely an idea, or an object, or a subjective experience, but it is a sum of the dynamic interaction of these three categories. We need to be present for art to "happen" for us, and, if you like, it is a certain *kind* of being present . . . an act of *faith*, just as someone picking up a pencil to draw what is in front of them does so in faith that they will either discover an order in the shapes depicted, or even create and project an order onto the assembled objects in the very act of drawing them. Looking at and interacting with art is an act of faithful reception, because we do so in the hopes that the artist has something they want to communicate, and/or in the hopes that the arrangement of shapes, colors, density, etc. will somehow register and click with that inner quest for balance that drives us.

Now that we have introduced faith into the equation, I'd like to use the preceding remarks as a springboard into the biblical materials. I believe that the stories we are about to comment on contain some truths about how we as Christian artists should appropriately handle our ideas and materials, and also some truths about the varieties of response we might run into.

We are going to look at examples from the Bible dealing with storytelling, mixed media, and performance/theater.

I believe each example breaks down, for the purposes of discussion, into three components. And I believe that our grasp of these components and their interrelationships will enable us, as Christians, to make art that is internally coherent and also dynamically relevant.

## YOU ARE THE MAN!

A careful reading of the books of Samuel reveals how the little things lead to big things in the lives of Saul and David. When David the king, living in luxury and safely away from the battlefront, spies Bathsheba, he embarks upon a course that involves adultery and murder. This was not the first time David had used his regal status to take what he wanted, regardless of who it hurt. Michal's first husband, Paltiel, followed her in tears when David summoned her to his side, collecting on an old promise made by Saul. But now David has fallen into grievous, deep sin with Bathsheba, and the prophet Nathan is given the task of telling David a story that holds up a mirror to his wrongdoing.

> The Lord sent Nathan to David. When he came to him, he said, "There were two men in a certain town, one rich and the other poor. The rich man had a very large number of sheep and cattle, but the poor man had nothing except one little ewe lamb he had bought. He raised it, and it grew up with him and his children. It shared his food, drank from his cup and even slept in his arms. It was like a daughter to him.
>
> Now a traveler came to the rich man, but the rich man refrained from taking one of his own sheep or cattle to prepare a meal for the traveler who had come to him. Instead, he took the ewe lamb that belonged to the poor man and prepared it for the one who had come to him.
>
> David burned with anger against the man and said to Nathan, "As surely as the Lord lives, the man who did this deserves to die! He must pay for

that lamb four times over, because he did such a thing and had no pity."

Then Nathan said to David, "You are the man! This is what the Lord, the God of Israel, says: 'I anointed you king over Israel, and I delivered you from the hand of Saul. I gave your master's house to you, and your master's wives into your arms. I gave you the house of Israel and Judah. And if all this had been too little, I would have given you even more. Why did you despise the word of the Lord by doing what is evil in His eyes? You struck down Uriah the Hittite with the sword and took his wife to be your own. You killed him with the sword of the Ammonites. Now, therefore, the sword will never depart from your house, because you despised me and took the wife of Uriah the Hittite to be your own.'

"This is what the Lord says: 'Out of your own household I am going to bring calamity upon you. Before your very eyes I will take your wives and give them to one who is close to you, and he will lie with your wives in broad daylight. You did it in secret, but I will do this thing in broad daylight before all Israel.'"

Then David said to Nathan, "I have sinned against the Lord."

Nathan replied, "The Lord has taken away your sin. You are not going to die" (2 Sam. 12:1-13).

There are certain dynamics to the chosen medium of storytelling that come into play as Nathan narrates. He establishes both a consensual and specific point of contact with David. David was chosen to be king from the life of being a shepherd. The anointing to regal status outflows from his shepherd life and experience. Nathan's story therefore establishes tension between the assertion of regal prerogative over a shepherd's poverty. Immediately there is a plot interest, because David is hearing two links of his own life experience (shepherd/ruler) set in dynamic opposition to one another.

Nathan says, in effect, "Do you recall what it was like to be a shepherd?" He then appeals to David's sense of justice: "What do you feel about this, David? Is this something that is right and fair?" Nathan's narrative not only convincingly draws upon agricultural and regal metaphors; it also provokes the right questions. It convincingly creates a context and then establishes ground for the hearer to dynamically respond to that context. Then, and only then has Nathan the storyteller earned the right to point out to David that the performance of David the king makes a mockery of David's heart as a shepherd, and also betrays his innate sense of justice.

Nathan was familiar enough with the incidentals of shepherding, and also the "dog eat dog" economics of how the rich treat the poor, to be able to furnish the story with a wealth of incidental detail. He is able through his art to effectively engage David's sympathy before confronting his soul. It seems worth pointing out that the biggest mistake we make in any form of Christian communication is saying "Thou art the man" before we have earned the right to be heard and have demonstrated a flexible understanding of the problem by "modeling" it; in Nathan's case, in an art form or media form.

All too often, we make the mistake of saying "Thou art the man" before we have demonstrated that we know what we are talking about in our confrontation. We can talk generally about "Sin"—but which sin? Are we content merely to label them, or do we know enough about people to be able to describe convincingly and sympathetically how a person gets into a situation. Nathan both understands the nature of storytelling and empathizes with individuals.

Jeremiah, on the other hand, had to confront an entire nation with its idolatry.

## GET DOWN TO THE HOUSE OF THE POTTER!

Jeremiah 18–19 uses the metaphor of pottery as a means of confronting the rebellious and idolatrous Israel with its sin. He drew upon his observations of a potter: someone who molds clay on a turning wheel, someone who is not afraid to radically reshape a pot if it gets out of shape, and someone who maintains control of the medium—and is not dictated to by the medium—as he works. Jeremiah, having drawn upon the metaphor of the potter to describe God's relationship to a rebellious and idolatrous Israel, goes on to talk about God's judgment coming suddenly.

Jeremiah has learned (by observation) what clay will do if left to its own devices. It will harden. It will be good for nothing. If Jeremiah had attempted to make his point with balloons or an ice sculpture, or even a story about a poor and a rich shepherd, it would not have quite been the same. He spoke publicly and publicly smashed a pot to make a statement about God's judgment on Israel. The first part of what he had to say drew upon his understanding of how a potter works. The second part of his insight drew upon his observations of what happens to clay when it hardens.

This was a dynamic gesture, made in full public view, that drew upon the prophet's acquaintance with a medium (shared with his audience) and also the prophet's acquaintance with the heart of God. This is theater/performance designed to challenge, provoke, and confront, with a view to getting these people to change. As such, it combined the fruit of contemplative observation with dynamic prophetic action. Jeremiah was aware of the properties of a given medium (and its potential, therefore, for metaphor and analogy), the character and concerns of God, and also the "state" of his audience, Israel.

In our first example Nathan knew enough about storytelling and the life of his audience to shape a convincing and convicting narrative. In our second example, Jeremiah was obedient to God and went to watch a craftsman at work and also to watch discarded clay harden in the sun. He also kept his ear and heart open before God so that he could learn how these observations could be turned into dynamic metaphors in his comments to Israel. Both Nathan and Jeremiah were deeply committed to both medium and audience. This deep commitment sprang out of their obedience to God.

For our third example we move to the Gospel of John. In John's account, Jesus commenced His public ministry by cleansing the temple. In order to explore this more fully we need to ask a couple of questions. What is the temple (at the time of John's narrative of Jesus' ministry)? What has happened to the court of the Gentiles, and what did the dialogue afterwards mean?

The court of the Gentiles had been established as an outer court into which all the nations would gain access to the true God. It had now provisionally been set up to accommodate the financial needs of the Jews traveling in for the great festivals. They needed religious money to pay temple tax, and so there were brokers in international currency there offering the coin of the realm to needy travelers.

People traveling long distances also did not want to drag sacrificial animals with them, and so handily enough there were some on sale there on the premises.

When Jesus went into the temple he did three things, according to John's account, that mark this as a threefold "event" very much along the Old Testament prophetic/Jeremiah lines.

**1. He drove out the animals.** Question number one: How could a good Jew or God-fearing Gentile make an appropriate sacrifice if there were no animals?

**2. He overturned the tables of the money changers.**

Question number two: How can anyone pay their tithe if all they have is "unclean" foreign currency?

**3. He asked the sellers of doves to take their cages and go.**

Question number three: How can a poor person approach God if the "dove" offerings, established for the pious who could not afford a larger sacrificial animal, are not taking place?

When Jesus was asked what right he had to do this, He replied that if they tore down this temple, He would raise it in three days. What he meant was the temple of His body, sacrificed in death, would be the only effective way of approaching God, replacing the need for sacrifices and temple ordinances. What they heard was Him talking about destroying a building that was the heartbeat of Judaism while under Roman occupation.

Jesus chose a very dangerous way of making a point, and as we can see, the whole thrust of Jesus' life and message hinges exactly on the gap between what He said and what the temple authorities heard. For Jesus' parabolic action to be ultimately effective, it would have to be initially misunderstood!

Jesus could have simply included some teaching about the temple passing away in some of his discourses. He could have simply paraphrased what was said to the Samaritan woman in John 4 about "spirit and truth." Instead, he engaged in a parabolic action which not only stressed continuity with the method and the message of the Old Testament prophets, not only revealed the true heart of God, but also set in motion a course of action that climaxed in His death and resurrection, thereby fulfilling the prophetic image hinted at in his dialogue with the pharisees, a dialogue that would not have taken place if he had not first cleansed the temple by physically driving out the animals, physically overturning the money tables, and talking to the sellers of doves.

Nathan could have kept quiet, but instead he used the medium of a story to confront David. Nathan could have said you are the one without engaging David first with a story.

Jeremiah could have simply told the Israelites how angry God was. Better still, he could have sent a messenger or a telegram.

Jesus could have done something spectacular at the temple (like jumping from the roof and surviving, as the Devil tempted Him to do) to demonstrate His power and authority and make His point. He would have gained His popular following—and probably shown the Romans a thing or two. Instead, he entered the temple, called the authorities criminals, and tore down the whole sacrificial machine from the inside out. As we read the entire Gospel we can see that He was offering Himself as a replacement for the temple and its system of sacrifice. We can also see, with careful reading, that the misunderstandings of the religious leadership in their dialogue with Jesus led ultimately to the cross, the very thing that would put Jesus' prophetic statements into effect!

When we look at the examples of Nathan the storyteller, Jeremiah the prophet, and Jesus (in this case, at least), who blended something like "performance art" and radical street theater, we can see that they were not detached, academic "armchair media theorists."

All three of them knew their medium and its context of reception. They also knew the heart of God, and they moved from theory to practice in front of a public that was repentant, or indifferent, or downright hostile. And in all three cases the work had its desired effect. David turned around. Israel was warned, and the Pharisees marked Jesus as a dangerous man who one day might have to be stopped.

What can we learn from these examples about sensitivity to media properties, audience, and context as we attempt to make socially and spiritually relevant art?

# LIKE A HOUSE ON FIRE

One of the main threads running through the previous remarks has been a concern with analogy and metaphor, and it is in that vein that I chose the title "Like a House on Fire." When I first heard this simile "explained" it had to do with how well people got along together. Another association that sprang to mind as I meditated on the phrase was the record in the Book of Acts of what happened on the day of Pentecost. From there I began to think about the contemporary concerns I hear expressed about the Church's mission in a pluralistic—or a "postmodern"—society, a society in which no one cultural style or description of reality predominates.

I hear talk about "local" theologies, meaning those theologies that arise out of practical struggle in the midst of a particular cultural and historical situation rather than simply being a theoretic imported abstraction. Some might argue against that charging that there is no longer an agreed-upon basis for "ultimate truth." In fact (they fear), there are as many "truths" as there are cultural expressions of them. It all becomes *relative*. I hear concerns about *syncretism*, which involves a blending of incompatible elements into an illusory "whole," or I hear charges of *piracy*, in which a Christian vocabulary ends up masking an alien agenda; say, an Oriental system of meditation, or a radically politicized analysis of a social situation and a call to action.

Of course, there are many grave risks in being a dynamic, expanding church in the midst of cultural diversity, as a close reading of the Book of Acts will reveal.

Just to give three linked examples: In Acts 13 the Apostle Paul argued with those who worshiped a particular religious tradition, a tradition that

Paul shared, incidentally; and if you want to know how Paul felt emotionally about the situation, read Romans 9. In Acts 14 Paul argued with those that wanted to worship the environment. To do so, he reached back to the general covenant God made with mankind through Noah in the early chapters of Genesis. In Acts 15 Paul and Barnabas went before the Jerusalem Council and defended their call to spread the gospel among the Gentile people groups, and in Acts 17, Paul argued with those who wanted to worship the intellect and its processes . . . and again he did so modeling the content of what he said within the context in which he found himself. He quoted their own poets and philosophers to them.

Obviously Paul believed that it was possible to communicate a ''pure'' gospel in culturally diverse ways. It was always a dangerous enterprise, and I believe that Paul's life and letters— and, incidentally, John's Gospel and epistles—wrestle with some of the key issues of keeping the gospel in context. It is the church's struggle to keep the gospel culturally and situationally relevant that stretches it creatively and, incidentally, should drive it back to its sources for the power necessary for the dynamic balance between purity and plurality.

Some thinkers have even argued that the gospel remains pure only in the act of being communicated from one cultural situation to another. Others might say that the gospel can only be universally relevant insofar as it first learns to be culturally particular. All in all, I think a reading of the New Testament reveals that our current issues of ''local theologies'' and ''cultural diversity'' and ''gospel in context'' had their first- century equivalents, and the solution then, as now, was to be found in the person and the work of the Holy spirit.

Well, so far today, under the umbrella of ''the house on fire,'' (to mix metaphors, and incidentally to come up with something I believe Andre Breton and Rene Magritte might have been proud of) we have linked together *charisma, creativity,* and *context.*

How does this tie in with our other lecture? What has this to do with art? Let me give you this quote from a book published in 1938:

> As at Pentecost, Parthians, Medes and Elamites heard the message ''every man in his own tongue wherein he was born.'' So we see Chinese, Japanese and Indian expressing Christianity's universal language, each with his own brush.[1]

We know from our previous talk that the arts take on very different roles and meanings in different cultural situations. Is there a way of thinking, talking about, and making art useful in the areas of cross-cultural communication and ''keeping the gospel in context?''

## WRAPPING THE ROOTS

At this point I'd like to use an image from a gardening practice. It has been said that to move a delicate plant from one soil to another, you must first "gently wrap the roots." It is important to protect the delicate parts of the plant while moving it from one soil bed to another. Now, what does "wrapping the roots" have to teach us when we think about the gospel, art, and cross-cultural communication?

I'd like to suggest that "the roots" of the gospel are not necessarily the first cultural forms through which it found expression, but the dynamic principles of "incarnational" living and communication that can be modeled and placed in many different cultural soils. Jesus is not a blond European or a Greek shepherd. He may have been depicted that way at certain times during the Church's missionary expansion. Sometimes we have the problem of getting the actual roots of the gospel, and the soil it was packed in that might still be clinging, a little bit mixed up. We identify the gospel with the cultural form in which we received it.

Now, this is fine as we seek to make the gospel "our own" in terms of obeying it and "living it out" in our cultural context . . . it is not so fine when we go to communicate across cultural barriers, and we end up passing on some of the cultural "soil" as if it were gospel root. The "roots" of the gospel are, if you like, a universally relevant message that continues to find culturally specific forms of expression. In fact, this dynamic of "incarnational communication" is much more accurately described as a "root" than is any aspect of a particular cultural form. Let me give an example.

In 1989 I attended a conference in Indonesia where many of the issues about the possible use of the arts for Christian communication in "developing world" traditional cultures were addressed. The Protestant church of Bali hosted us there and also served to dynamically demonstrate its own attempts to use the arts to express the gospel in Balinese terms. The Rev. Wayan Mastra, while traveling in Europe, observed how European Christians "Europeanized" the gospel in their church architecture, and also in their "taking over" of the pre-Christian mythological calendar for the purposes of the church celebration of Christmas and Easter. He returned to Bali and, in a similar way, Balinized the gospel, building a church along traditional Bali lines, with a roof shaped like a mountain and no walls so that the "outside world" of nature, plants, and running water could be seen and alluded to in preaching and worship.

Artists within the church began to use traditional dance and drama to tell the story of Jesus Christ, creator and celebrator of the beautiful natural world, who nonetheless came among sinners to rescue them from sin and spiritual bondage. They would make use of the Wayang Kulit shadowplay, beloved throughout large parts of Southeast Asia. The church workers and art makers would create new puppets and new stories in this art form, not only redeeming it, but also transforming it.

It was in the Balinese communion service and agape feast that the reclaiming and transforming of cultural elements was also markedly present. A traditional welcoming dance was done in which the dancers entered with lighted candles and used them to light other candles at the corners of the cross. A solo dance with traditional mask bore witness to a new life in Christ, and then gave opportunity for all communicants to join in the dance. Tea, flowers, and fruit were arranged upon a white cross design on the floor. Wayan Mastra says that the cross is ugly to the world, but beautiful to the Christian. Flowers and lit candles adorned the Balinese cross. Tea and fruit became communion elements. The Balinese cross not only reminds us of the sacrifice of Christ, but the foot washing during the service and the serving of tea and fruit remind us of our service one to another. Finally, the cross of fruit and flowers also powerfully reminds us of the redemption and the recreative transformation of nature that the Bible speaks about.

Let me summarize these points by referring back to our earlier image of "wrapping the roots." It has been said that to move a delicate plant from one soil to another, you must first "gently wrap the roots." We need to first ask ourselves, "What are the roots of what we are trying to communicate?" And then we need to be honest and ask if our "method of wrapping" sometimes damages the roots rather than protects them? If we confuse the cultural form in which we *got* the good news with the good news *itself,* we might end up wrapping the wrong thing or wrapping it the wrong way.

Very often our attempts to keep the gospel "safe" from contamination by, say, rock music or modern dance or even traditional folk media end up being a little like the actions of those cartoon characters who get chased up a tree and then saw off the branch they are sitting on so that no pursuer can come after them.

## BURNING BRIDGES

Along the same lines, it should be obvious that only a fool would set fire to a bridge while he or she is still trying to cross it. What are our "burning bridges" and how do they affect our attempts to communicate? Are they wrong ideas about the "universality" of the gospel? Confusion about the relationship between form and content? Confusion about the "neutrality" of the medium. Let me give some examples:
The English mystical poet William Blake wrote this:

> The vision of Christ that thou dost see
> Is my vision's greatest enemy. Thine has a great
> hook nose like thine.

Mine has a snub nose like to mine.

In crossing the bridge from one culture to another, one way of avoiding a fire hazard is to take note of what has to happen for our vehicle of communication to really and fully—if you like, "incarnationally"—communicate its message. It has to marry the chosen medium and its perceived meaning. It could be said that another aspect of "carefully wrapping the roots" in our cross-cultural artistic thinking is learning how to listen to what a particular medium or art form might mean or convey in a different cultural setting. Let me give some examples of problems that arose from ignoring these issues.

An American evangelical film shown to a Japanese audience resulted in a lot of questions about the American lifestyle, the amount of leisure time, and the abundance of home furnishings depicted. There were no questions about the film's "real" message. In some of the parts of India I visited it is considered rude not to turn your radio all the way up so that other people in the village can hear it. In our culture it would be exactly the reverse.

I experienced the problem of faulty "wrapping of roots" and bridge burning in a somewhat different way when I was in England several years ago. I was in York doing some research on the medieval mystery plays. One evening I went and saw a local church production of a "gospel musical" written by an American husband and wife songwriting team. The sincerity of the performers could not compensate for the very "transatlantic" feel to the whole thing, and in my opinion it simply did not translate very well. The next day I attended a High Anglican church service in York Minster. The choir came out and began to solemnly sing the Creed. Within moments the words were being swallowed up in the echo of the place with all its ornate trappings. The recitation had become an experience virtually without content, thanks to the ornate, cavernous setting. The truth of the words was lost in the style and the context of their delivery. The "roots" were wrapped in such a way by their environment that the life was squeezed out of them.

That we, even Christians, tend to make God in our own image is an almost commonplace assertion. Think back to the William Blake quote. It is not so well understood by some that there is a relationship between form and content in our communications, a relationship in which, if we are not careful, form modifies or even changes received content. Think back to my example of the echoes emptying the recited Creed of a clearly heard message.

There is much said today about the Incarnation as a model for understanding a correct approach to mission. There is emphasis on the concreteness and particularity of Jesus as a man with a culture and a history, and there is a challenge to earlier universalizing models: "Christ hidden in all religions" or, conversely, "Jesus is the answer, whatever the question, regardless of culture'' (the sort of sanctified steamroller approach). Of course, we know that it is written in the epistle to the Colossians and elsewhere that all things, whether in heaven or on the earth, were redeemed and cleansed through the Cross.

We also read of the defeat and the disarming of the powers. All well and good. However, I believe that the Bible tells us that it is precisely because of God the Father reconciling the world to Himself through His Son that we are able to think through the incarnational implications of communications across culture. The relevance of all this to our topic is that both missions across cultures and art making need to be considered in the light of both biblical example and biblical teaching. I would say from the example of Jesus and the teachings of the early Church that Christian communication is ''incarnational,'' taking into consideration the relationship between form, content, and context.

Think back to the early quote about the day of Pentecost and contemporary Asian and African painters. Think of how painting and sculpture combines inspiration and materials into a wholly new statement. Truly Christian communication and genuine art have a shared body of concerns in marrying material to ideas, form and content, medium, message, work, and intended audience. How much more should a truly Christian approach to art be sensitive to these issues?

## A THREE-BRIDGE MIND

I will suggest that in order to use the arts to glorify God and communicate across cultures, we have to build three bridges. What is a ''three-bridge mind,'' and how do we cultivate it?

The cultivation of this mind-set is properly the subject of another lecture. I can only make a few suggestions in closing.

It involves a threefold reaching out. Firstly, to our own artistic roots: In our culture, what characterizes the way the arts have developed for us? When we look at, say, the Church and the use of the arts in times past, are we able to identify ideas, trends, and characteristics?

## ICONS

The fathers of the early Church developed a marvelous theology of the transformed senses that formed the substructure and the rationale for their understanding of the place of the liturgy and the use of religious images that we know as icons. I say marvelous because at least they were thinking about it; and also, the worldview they operated in was more holistic and interactive (in the above terms) than the ''closed box,'' straight- line models of recent history. Icons provide for us a working model of one particular use the arts have been put to in the Church.

The arguments for and against icons are, of course, pertinent today.

The iconoclasts of the eighth and ninth centuries argued that it was inappropriate to try and depict the inexpressible via the image. The early church fathers who argued in favor of the icons argued analogously from the Incarnation, talking of Jesus as the image of God. The icon therefore (in the mind of the iconophile) not only gave an image for contemplative devotion, but also analogously "modeled" the relationship between the expressible and the inexpressible.

The medieval mystery play, on the other hand (to jump into another historical era and another art form), set out to provide a living book for the barely literate faithful. These plays took biblical stories from Genesis to the Book of Acts (and one or two Apocryphal and folk tradition sources) and strung them together to convey a relevant and concise narrative of instruction in the true faith. Many of the dramas brought the stories "down to earth" by depicting the situation in a contemporary style and setting. People could recognize themselves among the medieval peasants and shepherds. Everyone knew a "Noah's wife" who scolded and harangued her husband as he built the boat. Everyone could both identify with, and yet be amazed at, Joseph's lack of faith as he sharply questioned Mary on the truth concerning her untimely pregnancy. If the shepherds watching the fields by night could throw in one or two sharp comments about taxation and local landowners, so much the better.

These dramas, eventually staged by trade and craft guilds, served to inform and instruct. And they did so in surprising, funny, gripping, and dramatic ways. And they also rendered the gospel in contemporary terms, much like the European painters who dressed the biblical characters in European dress and sat them at a square, wooden table on wooden benches. If it can be said that the icons modeled a relationship, then the dramas mapped out the "narrative" of such a relationship for those that could not read. The dramas, of course, were not alone in their attempts to present a contemporary gospel for the community of the faithful. I have mentioned the visual artists.

It might serve us well to go back to the artists of that period and beyond to analyze their paintings as primary examples in the field of what missiologists call *contextualization.* I believe that there are some things we can learn from going back and examining the similarities and differences in motivation and concerns in the works of painters such as Giotto, Duccio, Peter Breughel the elder, Grunewald, and so on. We can explore everything from *what* they chose to depict to *how* they dressed and staged their characters. Were there underlying theological or moral concerns to their color values and spatial relationships, for example? Can we take an analytic approach similar to the analysis of various parts of a of a biblical passage (exegesis) and apply it to the various components of a painting?

Of course, I'm not suggesting that the underlying "meaning" of the experience of looking at a painting is reducible to an analysis of its components (see all of the above, especially the holistic systems stuff). I'm just locating some of the artwork and the intention of the artist in the culture of the time, and wondering whether or not we can learn from their methods and their models today.

Jesus was held up in the arts of the Church, not only as the prototypical expression of the inexpressible (icons) or the Saviour of the world (mystery plays). He was also held up via some of the art as the "Man of Sorrows," to be contemplated and *imitated.* The artwork was designed to provide visual cues for those systems of meditation that made use of the imagination, like that of Ignatius Loyola. Some of the art made within the Church was intended to provoke contemplative devotion to a view to imitating the character and qualities of the depicted Savior or saint.

These three intentions, contemplation of the inexpressible (icons), learning of the faith (mystery plays), and meditation with a view to action (artwork designed to spur one on in the "imitation of Christ"), characterize three uses our own church and culture have put the arts to.

All I'm suggesting is, please come to an understanding of the roots of our own culture and learn from it, good and bad, before attempting to reach out to another culture. If we can learn to build a bridge backwards into our own history, then we have gone a long way towards building the second bridge, a bridge into another culture, a culture with its own traditions, worldview, and art forms.

Someone raised the question of ccm—contemporary Christian culture and its categories of the *secular and sacred.* I am of the opinion, having glanced over what amounts to a "Christian industry" in the popular media, that the terms "sacred" and "secular" have more to with where your record will be slotted in a record store, and less to do with any enduring spiritual and moral values . . . regardless of what the salesmen for this mountain of product might try to tell you. I believe these categories are kept alive pretty much for the purposes of tapping into the reservoir of the Born-Again Buck.

It is possible, in my opinion, to build a "grass- roots/alternative" support base while trying to sell what you do to other Christians. It is possible, but we must proceed with caution for two reasons. We must firstly keep in mind that in a "post-Christian" culture like ours (as opposed to the other historical eras surrounding the icons, mystery plays, and so forth), the "Christian marketplace" is simply part of the real world we are trying to reach out to, or into, with our art. Regardless of the rhetoric, it is a business. Don't be seduced.

Also keep in mind that underneath all the labels, slipshod

categorizations, demographic projections, sacred hype, and born- again hucksterism, there are human beings—people—hungry and hurting for something. Your art form could be what they need, regardless of how they choose to categorize it. And let us remember that the "Christian marketplace" is simply one more symptom of a less-than-perfect world. Pretending it does not exist or laughing about it in our little "hipper than thou" cliques is not going to make it go away. Making your work available for those "who have ears to hear" is not the same as cynically exploiting the Christian community and its fears.

Tread carefully, but walk in faith. I say "tread carefully" because the idea of the arts in the Church is starting to catch on; churches are talking about art, and relationships between artists and churches are springing up here and there. We have to keep in mind that some sections of the "born-again subculture" have not really developed the maturity and discrimination of taste necessary for "testing all things, and holding fast to what is good" in the realm of the arts. An artist and a church committee can be in the same room at the same time and be talking past each other with their own presuppositions and set agendas.

We need some mind and heart expansion, flexibility,long-suffering, and tolerance in both parties for everyone to benefit (and God to be truly glorified) in this resurgence of interest in the arts for the Church. If a church pastor or committee has had its artistic tastes formed by the norms of the subculture, or is overly concerned with its particular goals and agendas, then its stated enthusiasm for the arts may end up being more a source of frustration for the artist. Of course, no artist should expect a "free ride" of nonaccountability when it comes to working in a church context. There is much ground to cover and many presuppositions to unlearn in clearing the way for the artist and the church to work in harmony in today's "post-Christian," agenda-driven society.

Going back to our earlier concerns with the "sacred/secular" terminology, the second point to keep in mind is that there are some parts of the world where the terms "sacred" and "secular" *do* have some relevance and potency. It is a mistake to look at the whole thing as a charade and dismiss it all as simply racking up record sales and riding in tour buses with tanning booths. If you intend to reach out into other cultures with your art form, then you need to recognize that within the worldview of some of those cultures the dimension of spiritual reality is taken very seriously. An important part of building a "three-bridge mind" is not to judge the spiritual realities evidently operative in other cultures by the excesses and dishonesties of our own.

Just as there are worldviews and philosophies that do not fit comfortably within our Western, post-Enlightenment framework, so there are also cultural and spiritual factors at work that give added weight and depth to the concepts of "sacred" and "secular." It would be foolish to dismiss them simply because some aspects of our own "sacred" culture have many of the hallmarks of a three-ring circus. Maybe you have seen the "Far Side" cartoon, in which one circus lion whispers to another that the lion tamer's gun is loaded with blanks. *"Precious friend, is your gun loaded with blanks tonight? Yes, I see that hand. Come on down. Your friends will wait for you. . . ."*

Anyway, luckily we don't have to be dupes for the marketing strategy, but neither do we have to be left vulnerable by our cynicism. The building of the third bridge will provide us with the insight to make true and appropriate judgment concerning the situations we find ourselves in. Our third bridge, of course, is back into the Bible and the heart of God. Here we find not only accurate guidelines for making these kinds of judgments, but also wonderful examples of creativity. We can come to understand the inner dynamics of how a parable works; how Jesus uses storytelling, exaggeration, symbol, and metaphor to communicate.

We can come to grips with the forms of the epistles and Paul's use of the Old Testament in application to the life of the new Church. We can move back and understand the symbolism of the types and shadows, the sacrifices, the tabernacle, the strange behavior of the prophets, and the full range of expression in the psalms. We can come to grips with the roots of metaphor, the placing of one thing as a reference to another in the intercessory prayers of Moses before God on behalf of Israel in Exodus. And we can begin to see that analogy, metaphor, intercession, reconciliation, and atonement are very close to the heart of the triune God and His dealings with this particular creation.

If we can grasp this—the reaching back into our own cultural roots, the crossing over to another culture, and the looking into the heart of God via His word—then we will have begun to build the three-bridge mind necessary for any real communication.

In closing, the early Bible translator William Tyndale says this, and I leave you with his words to further aid your meditation on the potential role for the arts in the church and the world:

> . . . though sacrifices and ceremonies can be no ground or foundation to build upon; that is, though we can prove nought with them, yet when once we have found out Christ and His mysteries, then we may borrow figures, that is to say allegories, similitudes, or examples, to open Christ, and the secrets of God hid in Christ. . . . For similitudes have more virtue and power with them than bare words, and lead a man's wits farther into the pith and marrow and spiritual understanding of the thing, than all the words that can be imagined.[2]

# 3

# Always is Never a Long Time

## *by Rupert Loydell*

**RUPERT LOYDELL's poetry, prose, and critical writings have appeared in hundreds of magazines in the UK, Europe, and America, and in many anthologies. He is a painter with many group and solo shows to his name, and he edits Stride Publications, which he founded in 1980. Rupert and his wife, Sue, live and work in Exeter, Devon, England.**

**In a religious age, the concept of spirituality in art is attracting attention. Rupert Loydell believes we should distinguish things that differ.**

# Abstract Art and Spirituality

On seeing a picture of the Virgin and Child, most people would readily pronounce it to be "religious art." They would be equally confident in deciding that a picture of a sixteenth-century nobleman should not be described in this way. It's far more difficult to categorize nonrepresentational art with such confidence. Significantly, there has been a good deal of talk recently about the "spiritual" aspect of "abstract" art. As it happens, both adjectives are rather slippery, and before discussing the question it's necessary to get a firm hold on them.

## ABSTRACT ART

1. The first point to understand is that art is a *language*. As such, it has its own history, vocabulary, nuances, and oddities. It needs to be learned. This doesn't negate the possibility of immediate appreciation, enjoyment, or learning from a work of art or criticism, but it *does* mean that you will probably get more out of art as you learn more about its context and intention.

2. The second point is my conviction, shared with many other professional artists, that *there is no such thing as pure abstract art.* All art depends on reality for its source material—whether that be observable reality (things you see) or the artist's emotions and feelings. This source material undergoes creative synthesis both through thought processes and material processes (i.e., paint, sculpture, etc.) to produce "art."

Not only is the source "real," but abstract art uses the same code of materials that all art uses. Imagine a line. No problem, you say. But there is no such thing as "a line" in the "real" world. A line is simply a mark we use to encode where, say, light and dark or two colours meet. It is a representational mark, a flat, two-dimensional scratch of dark on paper or canvas. It is the same mark whether it is part of a realistic image or a pattern.

It is easy to talk in general terms about "abstract art," but there are many different kinds of abstraction in art. We might refer to a linear series of art movements (Dada, followed by Surrealism, followed by Abstract Expressionism, followed by Pop Art, etc.), but the advent of Postmodernism makes such a survey unnecessary, for it gives us the freedom to absorb all stylistic and material-based conventions at will and thus allows us to concentrate on the general themes of abstract art instead of becoming bound up in history.

I also want to stay away from contextualization. This is of use to us when we try to understand art—and the study of art and culture is fascinating, but there are many ways of interpreting and reading art. I want to step right back to the artist and his or her intent.

So let's try and map out some areas of abstract art (many compartments will, of course, overlap):

1. Formal experimentation. Artists such as Kenneth Martin use chance in a "cold," logical way to arrange bands of colour. Many artists in the sixties looked at what happened when arrangements of certain colours or objects were grouped together in response to mathematics, chance, or taste. I believe much of this was (and is) tangential to art and ultimately a dead end. We must not confuse it with . . .

2. Using abstract art—often large-scale—to create emotional environments. Mark Rothko or Barnett Newman both, on the surface, appear to belong to group one in that they use stripes or swathes of colour against other colours or shades of colour. *But* if their work and writings are considered, neither were concerned with any formal arrangements. Both tried to engulf the viewer—by means of filling their area of visual awareness—and produce a certain feeling or mood. Many of Rothko's paintings are dark and sombre and inspire awe or melancholy. Others are restful; some lighter works sing of summer, of the sky, and plants in spring. Barnett Newman's work is often more "zany," using plastic colours in juxtaposition to unsettle and jar the viewer. This sense of emotion may often also be associated with . . .

3. Work which tries to conjure and share a response to a particular place. My own work, along with many British artists, concerns itself very specifically with how a place impresses itself upon us beyond the simplistic visual / photographic senses. How do we convey the smell of ozone at the sea, the constantly shifting waves, the sparkle of reflected light, the mood induced by wild moors or desert vistas? Much British art of the fifties—

artists such as John Piper, Graham Sutherland, and the St. Ives School of Peter Lanyon, Terry Frost, Patrick Heron, Barbara Hepworth, etc.—concerned itself with interpreting the landscape in this way. Often a "motif" may be used, a kind of code, such as Terry Frost's work with circles (indicative of the sun) and strange arced shape, which came from boat prows and the way mooring ropes hang. Peter Lanyon's work dealt with the feel of gliding—his pictures speak of clouds, sky, aerial views of the earth, and the ruggedness of Cornwall, where he lived. My own work takes motifs such as standing stones and the shapes of harbours, and uses those to speak of the strength and everlasting nature of God, the beauty of the earth, the wildness of creation; or harbours which become havens—places of safety, like the sheepfold in the stories told by Jesus, the Good Shepherd.

This landscape work often overlaps with . . .

4. Multiple viewpoint art. In many ways this is an artistic game, started by the cubists, which tries to (perhaps) show a person (in a portrait) from all sides, or in different moods such as anger and joy, or to depict all the movements of a dog's leg when it walks. In some of Picasso's jagged head drawings we see several noses—not because he can't draw, but because he was interested in both the side views and a head-on view. Francis Bacon's figure paintings are often considered gruesome, but a look at any photo of the author himself will show you that—for starters—he often looks like his paintings. Not all of mankind is created physically beautiful in any stereotypical way, and Bacon's sliding, smeared paint often captures the way someone twists their head, moves their jaw when they speak, flicks their hair; that is, it captures an essential mannerism or part of themselves rather than any photographic image. (After all, that is what cameras are for!)

5. Decoration. Sometimes—as in Op Art, much romantic painting, and many applied arts—the artist is interested only in pleasing the eye. This purpose may be found in all the categories so far, but sometimes it becomes the prime concern, although (of course) it may produce a different effect upon the viewer of the art. In this, of course, it resembles the work of artists like Rothko or Newman who, as we've already seen, use colour to induce emotion in the viewer.

I hope this survey will help you next time you look at art. Remember art isn't simply about what we see around us; it is about an individual reacting to and modifying their ideas and experience to create something new. After that brief introduction to abstract art, let's look at the concept of spirituality and how some artists and art critics use the term. How well does it hold up in context?

1. Much art is considered spiritual simply because it is an internal synthesis of nature (what is seen or felt in the world) and the artist's internal aesthetic thought process. That is, it is "interior" and subjective in nature. Both Kandinsky (who also developed a very acute and perceptive theory

of colour psychology [i.e., how we react to specific colours and colour relationships]) and Hans Hofmann considered an artist's output dictated by his "vision" (sense of colour and form) and "spirituality." But Hofmann quite clearly said in his writing: "Spirituality in an artistic sense should not be confused with religious meaning." He knew that what he called spirituality was simply "the emotional and intellectual synthesis of relationships perceived in nature, rationally, or intuitively." Hofmann was simply talking about a heightened aesthetic awareness, or what we might call "inspiration."[1]

2. A lot of modern art that is called spiritual is pantheistic; that is, the artist (or theologian) claims not only that God is present in everything, but that everything is God, and that therefore all art can show us God or is perhaps a form of prayer. Whilst not denying that God can use anything for his own end, the Bible quite clearly states that God exists separately, outside the world. I also believe prayer is both intentional and two-way (i.e., a conversation, not an artistic statement). However, underlying this concept is a truth: that much of what a human needs to be complete (something we'll consider later) is unknown and mysterious. I would agree that much art (whether abstract, figurative, or any other art form) deals with much that cannot be articulated in words. When we are moved by music or art, we are affected by something "beyond" ourselves that we cannot see. We may be soothed or angered, challenged or alarmed by this experience, which we may not be able to express in words. Much art has a "nonverbal" content.

3. Some art theorists believe that by deliberately focusing on this nonverbal content it is possible to allow God the room to speak. This is most manifest in the belief that everything mirrors God, most clearly seen in icons with their focus on saints, or Christ Himself, which are a figurative version of this. Within Catholic and Orthodox tradition they serve as an altar-image or mandala-like image for prayer. Although *icon* is derived from the Greek word "eikon" which simply means image, in its more orthodox sense it has come to mean an image that is sacred in itself and also in the way it depicts God through its images of Jesus, Bible stories, or the world itself.

Rupert Martin, who curated a touring show in the UK called "New Icons," says:

> The icon in this sense is a transparent window through which is revealed the artist's view of the nature and person of God through Christ. It is also like a mirror reflecting Him in the reality of the present world, a finite image in the materials of pigment, stone or wood, and thus an emblem of the Incarnation itself.[2]

This interesting show contained figurative

images—some very traditional images of Bible stories, a series of beautiful simplistic crucifixion scenes, new interpretations (parables set in twentieth-century landscapes)—and more abstract work: harsh Art-Povera wooden crosses assembled from found items, fragmented stone wall-sculptures with the cross delineated by the stones (i.e., the cross was the blank within the image), and cibachrome photos of sequential leaf patterns, the light through the leaf itself making a vivid natural image, precious within hand-crafted and painted white box frames. Here there is clearly a spiritual intent and artistic exploration, especially when thematically grouped. (The visitor was also given a lot of help by the expansive catalogue essay.) Is God necessarily present within, by, this work?

Andrew Bick is a young Christian artist who makes small wood and wax sculptures and believes that his work is part of a mystical contemplative tradition, yet with no recognizable icon connection. He hopes that through contemplation his sculptures may bring quiet to the viewer and create an inner space (the soul?) which the one true God might fill, or speak to.

These panentheistic ideas (God, since He created everything, is manifest/mirrored in all [but not present in a pantheist sense]) are a traditional and historical part of church history, but they steer close to both illustration (merely depicting) and pantheism itself.

4. There is also religious art, by which I mean art that is produced for church or deals with "spiritual" subject matter. Much of this is crass and commercial; much simply a hangover from ages past when art was frequently commissioned by the Church. Religious artists may still feel the need to use traditional subject matter. This doesn't mean there is any spiritual content beyond depiction of historical events.

On the plus side, there is—too great to detail here—a new movement of artists taking art back into the Church (as institution), both as functional object (communion cups, banners, table/altar cloths, furniture, stained glass windows) and fine art (sculpture, painting).

5. Finally, where I stand, there are many artists who consider themselves primarily "makers of art" who are Christians. Their art is a "spiritual" activity in just the same way as the work of Christian musicians, bricklayers, teachers, whatever. Our art is redeemed because Christ redeems the whole when he puts us into relationship with God the Father. Of course we also sin, and this will be in our art (I don't believe in "perfect art"!), but just as my art deals with my relationship to the landscape, it will—if I am honest and putting my self into my art—reflect my relationship to God. It may not preach, acclaim, or intend to convert, but it is part of my faith.

I want to finish by pulling some strands and thoughts together, some of which we've hinted at earlier, some of which are perceived as problems by the Church or Joe Public:

1. Many people have problems about content. There is still too much demand for verbal communication within abstract art. (Psychologists, sociologists, scientists, artists, and therapists of every kind have argued for nonrational activity and understanding.) But still we demand linguistic interpretation. Yet we all know that sometimes things are "indescribable." The arts can help us in this. God made the indescribable, He created emotions, and He knows all that we experience. If we open ourselves to experiencing art we open ourselves to a wide spectrum of healthy, challenging responses. Most of us have no difficulty about doing this with music (which also deals with the unknown/indescribable and uses a coded language of sounds). We must learn to do it with colour, shape, and form—just as children do until they are taught otherwise, with the oppression of representation.

This is not to condemn nonabstract art. I believe all art is "read" the same way by the informed viewer—i.e., one who is able to understand the pictorial mechanics of a painting (as was intimated by my opening remark regarding mark-making and the use of understood signs and codes). But different styles and ways of working will suit each artist. The medium must suit its content— an abstract painting must actually need to be abstract. If I want to put forward a cultural critique of, say, race relations, a photographic documentary work or even a lecture or book may work better than an abstract project. However, if (with the same subject) the artist wishes to convey feelings of (for example) how they feel when being discriminated against, abstract may suit.

2. A very influential error is the myth of artist as "genius." Despite believing that the arts are special and that some art is truly great and will speak for centuries to come, we must—as a church, a community of people (and also as society in general)—make room for our artists. Until we allow them off the pedestal they have been set on, we are holding them out of contact with reality and idolizing aestheticism. The artist is called to be an artist—a calling that is no better or worse (although at times a lot less practically useful) than that of a plumber. The Church must trust the artist to make art and try to learn his language, just as the artist must be prepared to enter dialogue. There must be trust all round. Just as a plumber may not be needed by all, a painter or sculptor may only speak to a few. This is fine—very little in this world moves everyone or is of use to everyone.

3. Finally (and it overlaps with our first point about content), art, including abstract art, helps us be complete. By expressing the inexpressible, it links us with God. Thomas Traherne, the seventeenth-century mystic and poet, made a very daring statement: For God hath made you able to create worlds in your own mind which are more precious to Him than those which He created.[3]

We are made in the image of God. Part of that is an urge to create, to make, and—just like God in Genesis—to see that it is good. We are called to do all sorts of things: to husband and harness the earth, to live justly and righteously, to be in communion with each other and God, to love our neighbour, and also to create and to re-create. Re-create has the same root as recreation. We must enjoy colour and shape for themselves, must take childlike (not childish) delight in what we, and each other, make.

Abstraction is not inherently spiritual (although if we feel we cannot know all about God, it may help us to express the inexpressible about Him). It does not contain God (although it may mirror or concentrate our mind on Him). But abstract art is part of God's gift of art to us, and it is one that enables us to share with each other and Him. Like the rest of creation it must be subject to the Bible and its rules, and it must not be idolized. It is part of our humanity, which the Bible says is God's most precious creation.

Appreciating art in general—including abstract art—involves using our senses, our imagination, and our creative intelligence. Thomas Merton shows how disastrous the consequences are if we fail to do so:

> In a word, then, it is our inability to really use our sense faculties, our imagination, our creative intelligence, that makes us slaves of slogans, arbitrary pronouncements, and party lines in art. And this servility, which is a rank infidelity to God the Creator and to the Sanctifying Spirit of Truth, has brought about the corruption of sacred as well as non-sacred art.[4]

He goes on to say we must consider the effect of bad art on society, the Church—ourselves, in fact:

> Let us realize that desire for a more living liturgy, a keener appreciation of theology and scripture, a greater awareness of the spiritual depth and contemplative possibilities of Christian life, cries out for the help that will be afforded by a sane and spiritual formation in sacred art.[5]

So art is part of our whole human-ness, our total redemption:

> Man is a living unity, an integrated whole. He is not sanctified just in his mind, or in his will. The whole man must be made holy, body and soul together, imagination and senses, intelligence, heart and spirit.[6]

# Raids on the Inarticulate (Poetry & Art)

I'd like to start this session on poetry and art with a quote from a poem by W.S. Graham. Graham lived in the Southwest of England and was friends with many of the St. Ives painters, including Peter Lanyon, to whom this poem, (*The Thermal Stair*) is addressed, following Lanyon's death in a gliding accident:

You said once in the Engine
House below Morvah
That words make their world
In the same way as the painter's
Mark surprises him
Into seeing new.[1]

The first thing to notice is the final phrase—"seeing new"—which I think tells us a lot about what the arts do. They enable us to get a different perspective on things and understand different viewpoints, hidden meanings, why and how people or things work.

Let's take one step backwards. Why should we want to understand one another? I think this—for us, the Christian church or community—falls under "loving your neighbour"—the basic rule for living (after the all-important "Love the Lord your God . . . ") that Jesus gave us, replacing (or fulfilling, simplifying) the legalistic Ten Commandments of the Old Testament. If we are to understand one another we need to understand each other in our full complexity—mind, body, and spirit. Man is more than a bag of bones; he is created in the image of God and has the potential of eternal life in communion with God and all the people of God.

So how do most people live? Dorothy Sayers, in her remarkable book *The Mind of the Maker* suggests that

> to the average man, life presents itself as a series of problems of extreme difficulty, which he has to solve with the means at his disposal. This is particularly disconcerting to him, because he has been frequently told that the increase of scientific knowledge would give him "the mastery over nature"—which ought, surely, to imply mastery over life.[2]

This was written in the 1940s, but it's clearly even more applicable today. The interesting thing is that subjects are becoming more and more specialized, and that communication between areas is, in fact, worse than ever. Only a holistic vision—which Christianity alone can provide—can root humanity in reality.

I don't want to suggest that artists have better answers than anyone else, nor that they are any more special. But I am trying to get at the motives for making art. Most art is an artist's answer to a certain problem—usually an emotional or metaphysical question, sometimes subconscious ones. You know, the biggies—love, death, sex, the universe, and everything, but also ones like, Why is the sky blue? or How come everyone loves the sea? or How can I explain to everyone how happy I am? These are real questions, real puzzles; and I believe by tackling them, artists, in the way they see anew, help mankind's gears run smoothly.

John Wilson, in *One of the Richest Gifts,* says,

> All artistic works are an expression of our common humanity, our creaturehood. They are a practical response to the way we are made and, like all God's gifts, are meant to be used to His glory. But it is a fallen world. . . .[3]

He goes on to discuss the fact that our aesthetic sense needs redeeming like all other parts of us—our whole being, in fact. But, he says,

> In His grace, love and wisdom, God has endowed men and women with aesthetic appreciation, imagination, skill, craftsmanship and artistic ability so that, even in a sinful world, life may be illuminated by shafts of truth, splendour, hope and joy. Even ungodly art may be valid and important for a deeper and fuller understanding of personal and communal life.[4]

So the arts help us unravel some of our communal worries, feelings, and emotions. They illuminate—shine a light on, help us see better—and they convey truth. Wilson is using truth with a lowercase "t" here, not the capital "T" we associate with God-given revelation, but a universal human truth within the workings of the world. This doesn't mean everything is nice, all sweetness and light. Truth hurts—and art may make us uncomfortable or uneasy, challenge and provoke, as John Calvin knew:

> The human mind, however much fallen and perverted from its original integrity, is still adorned and invested with admirable gifts from its Creator. If we reflect that the Spirit of God is the only fountain of truth, we will be careful, as we would avoid offering insult to Him, not to reject or contemn truth wherever it appears. In despising the gifts we insult the Giver.[5]

But if it's all about "truth," why are there so many art forms? How do art and poetry differ? Does someone like me—who works in both fields—use the same ideas and ways of working?

*No* is the short answer! Let's look at them in a bit more detail:

We're all used to words; we use them every day. Most of us in the Western world read, and we all talk. We are a verbal society. Our information—history, sciences, stories, our faith itself (through the Bible)—is conveyed in language. What makes poetry different? Well, let's get rid of some cliches—poetry doesn't have to rhyme, poetry isn't just short lines on a page, poetry isn't all about daffodils and dying princesses swooning under romantic moons. But let's hope that you knew that! Poetry is about compression and the heightening of language. The specific juxtaposition and interplay of what's written in a poem transcend the individual words to make the poem something special. That is, the poem as a whole is greater than its parts. It grabs the moment and changes it into a frozen splinter of time; a magic, memorable burst of lucidity.

Let me share with you one of my favourite poems—it's called *Snow*, and it was written by Louis MacNeice in the 1930s.

> The room was suddenly rich and the great bay-window was
> Spawning snow and pink roses against it
> Soundlessly collateral and incompatible:
> World is suddener than we fancy it.
> World is crazier and more of it than we think,
> Incorrigibly plural. I peel and portion
> A tangerine and spit the pips and feel
> The drunkenness of things being various.
>
> And the fire flames with a bubbling sound for world
> Is more spiteful and gay than one supposes—
> On the tongue on the eyes on the ears in the palms of one's hands—
> There is more than glass between the snow and the huge roses.[6]

I'm not going to run a critical workshop right now, but it's clear that the poem transports us from a fairly ordinary scene—someone looking out through a window at some snow—onto a "higher plane," where simple things such as peeling an orange are indicative of a greater questioning and action. I don't think it's entirely successful: the last line states and explains what the author is trying to say instead of letting the reader work it out from the poem. But the middle verse moves me terribly, that resigned sense of wonder at the vastness and much-ness of the world, rooted into someone's everyday home experience.

The interesting thing with poetry is that it has to cope with both the linguistic baggage of vocabulary—every word is definable and specific (in a dictionary sense)—and the musical sense of shape and form (rhythms, breathing patterns, rhymes, assonance etc.), which are abstract. Poets often claim to be surprised (like Lanyon the painter) by what they have created, been inspired to do. It is impossible here to get to grips with inspiration and the workings of the subconscious, which all artists and writers—along with craftsmanship—rely on. There is a sense of exploration and venturing into the unknown, with only language to help . . .

T. S. Eliot describes this quandary in part of *The Four Quartets*:

Trying to learn to use words, and every attempt
Is a wholly new start, and a different kind of failure
Because one has only learnt to get the better of words
For the thing one no longer has to say, or the way in which
One is no longer disposed to say it. And so each venture
Is a new beginning, a raid on the inarticulate
With shabby equipment always deteriorating
In the general mess of imprecision of feeling,
Undisciplined squads of emotion.[7]

The next passage deals with the idea of not being unique, of only restating what other writers have done before, and better, but he knows his calling and must obey: "For us, there is only the trying. The rest is not our business."[8]

Language is a living, changing thing. It is specific at any one time, but it changes—words become archaic or change their meaning. They may carry cultural overtones for certain
age-groups; a poet does his or her best to weld them into language that transports and informs. Language is where the most information and specific themes, discussions and theories can be conveyed; poetry is often a way to the emotional, felt, human side of those specifics—it resolutely tries to get to grips with the inexpressible.

Painting and the visual arts also grapple with the inexpressible. Just as poetry must change the words into a greater whole, so must painting transform a series of colours, shapes, and lines. Over the years we have set up a language-based cultural scaffold (art history) and safety net (criticism) that have stopped us actually looking at art itself. We have contextualized works of art and reduced them to footnotes for discussions on sexuality, history, sociology, and personalities. Let's get back to the work itself and what the artist has to work with.

He has what he perceives with his five senses (for all we know in this world is what we have received in this way) and what he feels emotionally and intellectually. The feelings, plus sensory input, synthesize to make art. This relies on codes of light/shade, warmth/cool, and texture/line, surface patterns, shape, etc. There is no way painting can aspire to the specifics of, say, MacNeice's poem earlier. We could have a painting of a person in a room staring at the snow; we could feature an orange being peeled, the fire, the petals, but we can only hint at the wonder of the poem by subtle drawing of the person's face.

There can be no linguistic discussion (apart from perhaps the title). This, for me, is where abstraction comes in. Like music (which for some reason people can often cope with easier than abstract art), abstract art can move us to a sense of wonder, awe, despair, joy. . . . It would be easier, and perhaps a more suitable idea, to express the wonder and confusion of MacNeice's poem in an abstract. I might choose to introduce pictorial elements—flowers, oranges, fire—if I felt these specifics were needed. But hopefully we don't want to either illustrate or try and retell the poem; we simply want to express the emotion it produces in us.

Like the poem, the work must suit its own medium. It must be only expressible in the paint it has donned. It must use every nuance of colour, tone, and line to move the viewer (and initially the artist) towards some sort of destination. Just as words gather together, paint changes in context. I, like most painters, do not plan a painting in my head. It isn't a dot-to-dot, fill-in-the-gaps thing. It is an ongoing process, the disadvantage—compared to writing—being that a single brush-stroke changes the whole canvas, and there are no written drafts or earlier versions we can return to. The painting is only a painting—that is all a painting is meant to be. It may exist for the painter and only the painter, or it may speak in a universal way to thousands of people. Whichever extreme, it must be a painting as a painting, and not a tract, a piece of propaganda, or a poem disguised as a painting.

If you'll forgive me, I'd like to use a triptych of paintings and sequence of poems as an in-depth example of what I'm trying to get at. I say forgive me because they are my own work—but I think I'm on safer ground here than dissecting someone else's work. Incidentally, I don't think this kind of criticism is that helpful to the work itself—analysis tends to dull the sensory reception of work by the viewer/listener/reader. But let's give it a go.

Both pieces of work are called *Quartet;* both are about Easter. There are three paintings (the quartet refers to the shape of the paint, not the number of canvasses) and twenty-two poems. Each is designed to work separately; that is, the paintings aren't illustrations; neither are the poems any kind of explanation of the pictures! Having said that, the work was all done around the same time and relied on the same ideas and thought processes.

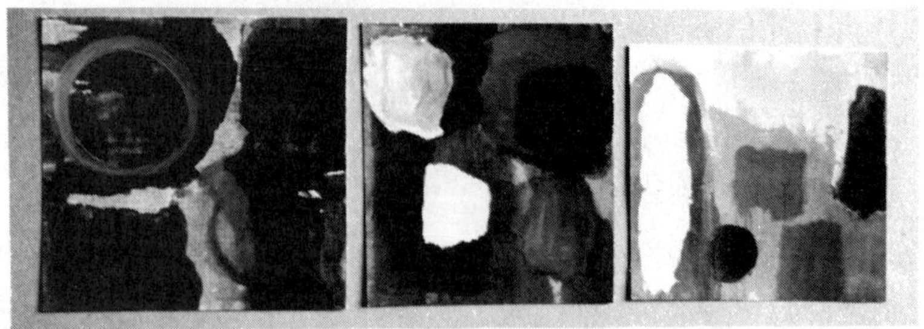

The first painting, which is fourteen inches square, is called *Shroud.* The title obviously is a big clue, as is the subtitle of the work, *An Easter Sequence.* The grey shape on the left is reminiscent of a body shape—it is broken ("broken for you")—and the picture hints at a cave in a landscape (green hills against a sky).

The second painting is called *Brief Sighs* and is also fourteen inches square (when hung together the work has picture three in the centre of one and two). Purple dominates the spectrum here, the colour of mourning. There is a cross intimated at by the thin paint between the heavier sections (there is also a series of monoprint studies with the cross very much to the fore). The circle is a sign of wholeness, but here there are three circles—one partially hidden (bottom right) behind paint. I wanted to hint at the Trinity and the idea of God and Christ being separated ("Why hast thou forsaken me?").

The final painting is called *A Miracle Arrives* and is two inches higher (fourteen by sixteen inches). Here is the Resurrection—the moment when the Spirit starts to breathe life anew into Christ, and mankind has the chance to be saved and healed. The red and orange burst through the colours.

Now all this isn't obvious, and it isn't a sermon, but it's there, subliminally hinted at. Primarily, though, this is a work of art—with balanced colours, forms, and shapes. Pleasing to the eye (or some eyes!) and a "good piece of art." In fact, it was shown at Greenbelt in 1987, and I was honoured to sell it to a man who had never bought a piece of art in his life, but felt moved. He had understood what it was about.

The poetry sequence is more complex, as you would expect from my earlier statements. It allows the narrator (writer) a voice, it offers several viewpoints, and it has several themes running through it. (Incidentally, each poem is designed to be a poem in its own right, and many were published on their own). These themes, or ideas, are:

1. The four seasons
2. The four elements: earth, wind, fire, and water.
3. The four suits in a pack of cards (and kings, queens, jokers, etc.).
4. The idea of quarters gradually being drawn together to make a whole, just as elements fuse in creation, the year is composed of the seasons, and a pack of cards is useless with, say, the hearts missing!

So let's start:

**1.**

Four corners
to this picture
Each overlaps and tells
a different story
The reasons seem the same
the edges blur
You are
taking my time
up and I
need reasons
Stealing the life
that I wanted
These colours
have run
I don't like
the composition
The abstract
chances take
all reason
The fragments
must be one
A quartet
perhaps—
within
the same frame
Tie the knots
tight and
hold on

We fall apart
together
taking time
to feel the reason

*"Four corners" refers to the paintings themselves, starts the sequence with the idea of brokenness, and carries a subtext of the four Gospels (which tell the story of Christ).*

**2.**
**EARTH**
For a time
your slow learning
your dull lives
Your disbelief
*
For a time
the deathly hush
the silence
Your fault
*
For a time
I would have loved you
but not now. Caught out
Your forgetfulness

*EARTH. The poem is Christ speaking, challenging (and angry with) the world.*

**3.**
The seasons
twine their
annual
decline
from yesterday
to a promise
foretold

*The seasons idea, with overtones of prophecy fulfilled and eventuality of both the way the world had to be saved and the way nature works in its annual cycle.*

**4.**
Take time
to learn
tightrope

Despair
never finds
its balance

*Hope.*

**5.**
I meet
someone
We've written
before but
in the flesh
is strange
We condense
and change
our previous
imaginary pictures
start to meet
again. You
meet someone

We constantly change our ideas. This can be a good thing—we should be open . . .

**6.**
**SUMMER**
Early sun
days and
hazy nights
offset
my chaos
at moving
Move mountains
and
waters flood

*SUMMER. The first season, but water is also present here in the tears of the poem. Written at a time of moving house (which I hated). Christ's mission was a major upheaval, the major moment in time . . .*

**7.**
Trust
is the only
ace we hold
Kings
and queens
are out to lunch

the joker
turns up trumps
all too often
Like
a pack
of wild beasts

*Cards. Trust equals faith. There's a pun on pack (animals/cards).*

**8.**
**AUTUMN**
Take time
to fall
apart
You said always
meant never
Take time
to tie these lines
between
You said always
Knots tighten
in my stomach
Take time
Toss it away
Casual
Juggle
The days
get shorter
I
spin
down
to
die
Crisp leaves

*AUTUMN. ''Fall'' to you guys. The second season. There are hints of Christ realizing what he has to do. Also about relationships, false promises. Puns on knots/ties.*

**9.**
Ghost talk
and never
no more memory
I say
you can
tell me something

The last thing
you lost
Merely dying

*Plea to not just die, unsaved.*

**10.**
Catch hold of quarters
of quarters
and tell
me a rhyme
Take hold of silence
of silence
and sing
for all time
Wait, there are reasons
are reasons
to give
to your soul
The reason is quartered
is quartered
the answer
is whole

*Quarters—the painting again. Grab/study the four Gospels; they tell us all we can know about Christ. Silence equals contemplation, singing equals praise/worship. There are answers to the questions (questions the last poem suggested you ask). This is a poem to the reader, not about Easter as such.*

**11.**
**WIND**
on my cheek
the only cooling
while I'm hung here
The earth
unhinges itself
from my care
I am dust
blown into
dark corners

(later
the visiting breath
that gives life)

*WIND—first element poem. Christ on the cross. The wind is also a symbol of the Holy Spirit.*

**12.**
Stone robes
in a cold tomb
Monumental
slates
Granite
Carve
this name
high
and watch
time
erode it
not at all
Polish this
stone
and find a name
to work
magic with

**13.**
The shaken snowstorm
whirls around
plastic figures
Cheap universe
for sale (and us
shivering like fools)

*Snow. We are the fools who killed the Saviour.*

**14.**
**FIRE**
I would have called down
an end to this
but for you
Wild fire to
swallow men whole
I have had my
very self burnt
skin grafted
on to loss
You turn away

from my wounds
The scars will
never heal
The glazed pot
rolls from warm ashes
blown clean
made whole

*FIRE. Element poem. Christ talking again. The cross was a very real physical torture He had to endure. He was broken for us. The Resurrection is hinted at by the reference to pottery—raku firing.*

**15.**
**WINTER**

Snow shine
at night
outlights
the
temperature's fall
I hold you
warm
and breathe
Mist
condenses
around your face
Your smile
a shattered moon

*WINTER. A love poem, continuing the tradition of secular/sacred love.*

**16.**

Quartered
cut up and
spent here
and there
Divided and fallen
until you pick me up
and reassemble whatever
you find  or need
You will find me
in your stories
your talk, every
element has traces
Symbols disregarded by science
Take water, earth, and spit

Fire to bake matter, create
Now you are to blame too
Assemble these splinters
Take these elements for a time
Take care. Be wise. Take time
Look which way windward

*God is everywhere in our world. We have to do the looking and searching. The four elements are mentioned here as part of creation.*

**17.**
Love not
the world
Love knots
the world
Love knots
the words
Tangles before
the darkness
Suddenly
feeling alive
Fill the shelves
and swallow whole
We do not deliver

*We have to rely on God; only He can heal. We are renewed—the shelves are full, we are whole.*

**18.**
**GREGORIAN CHANTS**
This music
walks on air
all the way
to heaven

*A sanctified sort of art . . .*

**19.**
**WATER**
fills the gaps between the
chaos my father left as you
We splash it for symbols
drink it to survive
Poured it spills
to the ground. I am death
for this moment. I swallow
that emptiness you fear

I am a
stagnant waterfall
falling still

*WATER. Seas, baptism. Water sinks away into dry ground—idea of death, which Christ has conquered (swallowed). Jesus is the living water, a permanent, constant source. Contradiction/wordplay of falling still, still falling.*

**20.**
Kaleidoscope
rainbows—
the dove
descends
A million
fragments
Birdsong
shatters
silence
The circle
merges
We shape
the world
It moulds us
if we do not
A quartered
love heals

*"Rainbows"—idea of many colours in the paintings, God's promise to Noah. "Dove"—Noah, and Holy Spirit. "Fragments"—healed. We have to change/resist the world, or we get moulded.*

21.
SPRING
Steering
for a promise
that flowers
in a desert

*SPRING. Hold to God's promises.*

**22.**
Always
is never
a long time
Caught
inside these

forces
take a
wild cut
Enough
A heaven
asking questions
of itself
Not limited
by
nothing

*Heaven. Eternity for most of us holds both fear and wonder; we don't understand the idea of forever. The "wild cut" refers to the pack of cards. "Asking questions"—all questions can be answered in God. We are free if we are in relationship with the Father, through Jesus.*

Now, I think that although I may have helped you get some ideas of what I was doing in those poems, you have been denied the pleasure of listening to the words work for you as poetry. I also think you'd have enjoyed unraveling the themes for yourselves, and you probably have found connections and ideas I haven't thought of. I have to say that although I started with the various themes and ideas in my head, I didn't map out a plan of poems to write. Much of this interpretation was done after the poems were written, when I got to grips with what my subconscious had written!

So two very different ways of saying similar things. The poetry is clearly better as a means of "talking" and "understanding" some of what Easter is about. But although I can't talk about my paintings like I can the poems, that's because—as I said earlier—the paintings are paintings. I know they overlap thematically, but they express something that can only be told nonverbally. They are pigment on canvas, colours and shapes in a certain set of spatial relationships.

The urge to create is a God-given one that all of us possess to some degree or other. There are many ways to create. Each must choose, each must find for himself what God has planned for him and how to use their creativity. This creativity is given for our pleasure as well as for our education and witness. It deals with the (again, God-given) complexities that we face if we live our lives to the full. Just as sex is to be celebrated within marriage, colour, language, music, and theatre help us to be alive, exploring the world we've been given to live in.

John Wilson, in conclusion: "The Christian does not have a narrow, bigoted view of the arts which can illuminate and enrich his life. All things are his."[10]

Let us not look a gift-horse in the mouth, but accept it with thanks and praise.

# 4

# Artistic and Spiritual Priorites

## *by*
## *Rick and Brenda Beerhorst*

**RICK and BRENDA BEERHORST live in Grand Rapids, Michigan. Rick, an NEA Fellowship recipient, is known for his paintings of biblical narratives in contemporary settings. Brenda divides her time between free-lance art and collaborating with Rick.**

# Artistic and Spiritual Priorities

RICK: We come to you in complete weakness and trembling today. Often, before we give speeches like this, we feel very insignificant. I've been sitting in on some of the other seminars, and the speakers are really good. I was beginning to wonder, "What am I doing here? I'm not as good as these other speakers." Then I saw a guy wearing a T-shirt that had on it a verse from Zechariah (4:6), " 'Not by might, nor by power, but by my Spirit,' says the Lord." That verse encouraged me, and that will be the crux of our talk.

Brenda and I met each other in 1985, and we've been journeying together the last six years. We're going to tell you what the Lord has brought us through and how He's changed our way of seeing things.

But first we have our own private stories. I grew up in the suburbs of Grand Rapids, Michigan, and my family wasn't necessarily culturally inclined. We listened to Muzak, not Haydn. But when I was young, I started to find out what I was good at. Other people, when they're young, find out they're good at sports or getting good grades. For me, I was good at art, good at drawing. The first things I remember drawing were cats around the house and cartoons like "Peanuts." Then I drew my mom, just with an ink pen, and it was easy. I just sat down and did it. And then a wave went through my family; they said, "Whoa, here's this little kid, and he can draw!" And I felt really good about it. And I was excited! So I started doing lots of drawings when I was in school, especially cartoons of Snoopy and the Red Baron.

BRENDA: Like Rick, I started drawing as a young child, and by the time I was a teenager I really identified myself as an artist. I was introverted and lonely, and I had an eating disorder. I was also cut off from my peers. But one thing that connected me was whenever someone needed a poster or someone to design a float or program cover, I would help out. I was the artist of my class, and I had a lot invested in that. My whole self-esteem rode on that identity

After high school, I went to Kendall College of Art and Design in Grand Rapids, Michigan, and art was still my life. Without art I didn't know who I was. I wasn't a Christian at this point; I was raised Catholic and I really didn't know the Lord. We went to church, but it didn't mean anything to me. My identity was in art, and it worked for me. I got great grades at Kendall and I made a lot of friends there.

RICK: I found my identity in being an artist, too. When I went to college, it all started coming to me in one rush: classical music and underground music. I went to a Christian college, Calvin College, in my hometown of Grand Rapids. The Christianity I experienced there was very dry—at least in the circles I was in. It was the kind of place where we were all supposed to be Christians and we all assumed we were Christian, but we never really talked much about things of the Lord. My heart kept shrinking smaller and smaller, and my brain was getting bigger and bigger; I was getting open-minded, or so I thought.

In college one book in particular hit me: *My Name Is Asher Lev* by Chaim Potok. It's about a child, an artistic prodigy, growing up in a Jewish home where art isn't accepted. He struggles in his art, and he's misunderstood, but some key people in New York, where he lives, discover him. The book ends with his having a big show in the most important gallery in New York. So that was my picture of success.

By the time those four years were over, I was really into beatnik literature, like Jack Kerouac and Allen Ginsberg. I got into this crowd where we were all hip, we dressed cool, we all spoke cool, we all hated our fathers, and we listened to the Velvet Underground. (I still do, once in a while.) I started to cut myself off from my family and anyone else who didn't dress like me or listen to my kind of music. This isolation took me out of Christian fellowship, and I backslid quite far.

Like most twenty- to twenty-two-year-olds, I had this notion of impending success. Once I read the story of Johnny Cash—he just knew in his heart someday he was going to be famous. I had the same thing. Difference is, of course, Johnny Cash is famous, and I'm not. I'm thirty-one now, and not famous. Anyway, I dropped out of college for a while because I thought I'd be famous. It was getting boring, and Bob Dylan never finished, so why should I? I hung around Grand Rapids for a while, and then I went to the place where everyone goes to get famous: New York City. I thought I'd just shoot right to the top because I was a genius.

However, right before I moved to New York, I went to see my brother, who lives in Holland, Michigan. I loved him even though I thought he was a square. I went to him and said, "Ray, this is what my life is," and I told him everything, right up front. And he didn't condemn me. He just said, "Rick, are you a Christian or not?" That simple. If you're a Christian, you live a certain way, and if you're not, you should just drop the title. I drove back home and I knew he was right—totally right.

So I started reading the Bible and other books my brother gave me. And I started to think that God was going to use me to save all my friends. I started with my girlfriend at the time, but she didn't want to hear it. We argued, and that relationship ended, and I was a broken man. Then I started sharing spiritual things with my best friend. All I knew was rhetoric, and I thought if I had a good enough argument and read enough C. S. Lewis I could convince him. So I came in with my arguments. My friend, who was really much brighter than I was, would get red-faced and fuming. I thought I was actually getting somewhere! I mean, prophets get stoned, right? Finally he blew up at me and said, "Rick, you used to be so beautiful; now you make me sick. I hate you and I hate your God." It just knocked the wind out of me; I didn't have another word to say. And I went downstairs to my room and fell onto my bed and cried myself to sleep like a two- year-old. That was the bottom for me. I had no friends; I was all alone.

The Lord brings us to places like that—wilderness places. You've all been there. But the wilderness is your friend, not your enemy; the Lord brings us to that place for a reason.

BRENDA: Both of us were very success-oriented. I dreamed of working for Hallmark. At the end of my three years at Kendall I applied to Hallmark. I got pretty far in the process, and I was feeling very confident, but finally I got notice that they didn't need me. And I was crushed, to say the least. After that I had a really long struggle. I couldn't find a job. I thought I would get a job at an advertising agency and wear nice clothes, and I ended up getting a job in a screen-printing place and wearing dirty jeans. It was terrible. So my self-esteem started to fall apart. Everything I had based my life on so far began to crumble. I was embarrassed to see people because I was working a crummy job, and then I got laid off and was even more embarrassed and depressed.

I still didn't know the Lord, but I started to search for Him—for something. I hung around Christian bookstores and tried to find a book that would tell me what life was about. I looked all over and I couldn't understand a thing—these books didn't make any sense to me. I finally found a daily devotional by Corrie Ten Boom, and I started reading that along with my Bible, but it didn't connect for me. At one point I was so down I was going to commit suicide. Finally I said, "Lord, I can't stand my life anymore. You take it." And after that things started to change. I got a better job, and I really felt the love of the Lord flowing through me.

Good things happened to me for about six months. After that, because I wasn't discipled, I drifted away. My life started to get empty again. I became dissatisfied with my job and thought maybe I should pursue fine art instead of commercial art. Fine art seemed a higher calling—more real, more interesting, cooler people. So I went back to school and pursued a bachelor of fine arts degree in painting.

I started painting angst-ridden paintings. They were really dark and disturbing, and I thought they were really cool, and so did a lot of people that I knew. I was working things out through my paintings, but the more I dug into myself, the more I just wallowed in darkness. I was getting more and more depressed. Finally I recommitted my life to Christ. I went to InterVarsity, and spiritually things started picking up. But artistically I was falling apart. I didn't know what to paint anymore because every time I started to paint I would get depressed. Sometimes it's really easy for young people to paint these angst-ridden paintings about life. It's easy to make a strong statement when you paint about darkness, but how do you paint joy and love without it seeming trite and superficial? I had produced a lot because my work was self-involved, focused on things that were troubling me. But I wallowed in my troubles instead of working through them. As I grew close to the Lord, my artwork became harder to make.

After I graduated with my bachelor's degree in fine art, I couldn't paint anymore. Every time I sat down to paint, I'd just get frustrated. I'd rip my drawings up. Everything bad about me came out. I had a temper tantrum every time I tried to paint.

RICK: She's not kidding; she really did. It was miserable to be around her.

BRENDA: Yeah. Rick and I knew each other at this point and were dating. But even after we got married I was still having this block, and I knew I had to paint because it was the only thing I knew how to do. I identified myself as an artist, and then all of a sudden I couldn't do it anymore, and then I didn't know who I was. And I'd see my friends and they'd say, "Well, Brenda, what have you been working on lately?" and I'd say, "Oh, I've been painting a little." But I was lying; I really wasn't painting at all. I began to wonder if I was going to be one of those people that get a bachelor's degree and never make art again.

RICK: It was really hard for me during that time, too, but my wilderness was different than Brenda's. I never had a problem making art. So I'd say to Brenda, "Honey, you've just got to have discipline." I had all this great advice: how we'd make time once every week for her to draw or paint. But when the time came, we'd get into a big fight and I could soon tell I wasn't helping her. There was a missing piece, and I didn't know what it was.

BRENDA: I was in the wilderness for a long time. For two years I didn't make any art, and it was really a difficult time for me. People asked me what I did, and I'd say what job I had then, like mental health work or whatever. People I knew kept asking how my art was doing. Finally I came to the point where I wasn't lying anymore. I wasn't saying, "Oh, I've been painting a little." I finally said I wasn't making any art.

That was tremendously humbling for me. I had a lot of pride in that area, and to say I wasn't making art anymore was like saying I'd given up. I was humbled and confused. All of a sudden I couldn't make art anymore because every time I tried I turned into an ogre.

I called out to the Lord a lot. I kept praying, "Lord, if you want me to make art I'm going to draw for half an hour every day." So I'd try that. I'd sweat bullets for a week and draw for half an hour, but I hated it. Finally I said, "Lord, what are you trying to tell me? Do you want me to quit making art?" At this point I realized I had put art as my salvation; art was how I found out who I was. Once I became a Christian I didn't need art for that anymore. The Lord was saying to me, "Brenda, can you still be okay if you can't make art anymore?"

Last year at Cornerstone [1990], I was talking to an artist, Janet Cameron. I told her, "I haven't been making art for quite a while and I don't understand why, but I think it has something to do with the Lord. He's trying to teach me something and I don't know if I'm ever going to make art again, because I think art was an idol in my life. My identity was not in Christ, but in art."

Janet was the first person who ever understood what I was saying. She said, "You know, our God is a jealous God, and He won't let anything be in our life before Him."

And I said, "Yeah! That's it! Finally I'm starting to understand what's happening to me." The Lord was taking my art away because He loved me and He wanted me to see that He can love me without my making art. People can love me if I'm not making art. That was a big lesson for me because I thought my art was the only reason people liked me. When that was stripped away I found out people still cared about me, people still liked to be around me, the Lord still loved me. I had nothing to prove; Christ alone made me worthy. It was a whole revelation to me.

When you're a Christian and are seeking to walk with the Lord, He's going to change you whether you like it or not. Well, God made it harder and harder for me to make art that didn't glorify Him. Finally I realized if I was ever going to make art again, I wanted to do it to glorify the Lord.

In the last year the Lord has been leading me back into making art. It's been a slow process, but it has felt right because God is taking my hand. It's fun again. And it's exciting, because it's not something I went after. It's God bringing me little jobs—drawings for churches, commercial things. It has really surprised me because I believed that I would not make art anymore. I had given it up completely. I had said to the Lord, "I don't care, I'm never going to make it again if that's what you want." Now he's slowly bringing it back.

RICK: The Lord brought us to a place where we sought Him with all our heart. And He continues to do that.

Brenda and I spoke earlier about how we had our identities in our art and how we started to see God's love for us was more important than what we were doing. Right now we want to talk about how God helps us when we're in the hard places.

After Calvin College, I went to art school: grad school at the University of Illinois in Champaign-Urbana. There I learned that you do art to express yourself, and if somebody else understands it that's wonderful, but you're really just making art for yourself. Because I was a pretty nominal Christian, I absorbed all that.

Yesterday I talked about how I wanted to be a success and show my work at galleries. Well, the Lord closed that door again and again for me. So my first job, because I wanted to make art for a living, was to make murals for an Italian restaurant in my hometown. The owner showed me what he wanted, and I said, "Okay, I can do that." When it was done, he liked the painting, and so did other people, and he paid me. It was amazing how good it felt.

BRENDA: When the gallery thing fell apart, Rick started to think, "Well, if I can't get into a gallery, I'm going to paint for the poor." I think this was a real turning point in his life. The mural he painted for the Italian restaurant gave him this idea to paint murals for homeless shelters. The Lord gave him this idea, and for the next year he spent a good portion of his life downtown drawing street people, the homeless, drunks, and prostitutes. He met a lot of people that he incorporated into his murals.

The murals are biblical narratives of Jesus set in contemporary settings. One was on the Triumphal Entry into Jerusalem, and he had Jesus riding a donkey down Division, which is a bad street in our city. And all the people behind him were street people. These people got to see themselves in a good light, and it was edifying for them. They point themselves out in the mural and are very proud of it.

I think the Lord really honored that, because instead of trying to get into a gallery, Rick took a step of faith and worked downtown on a tentative income. Our income came from gifts people gave to the project, and a woman helped Rick get a small grant to finish the project. That project was a turning point in Rick's life as far as art goes: he learned to stop pursuing it selfishly and to give his talents over to the Lord.

RICK: I heard this story Mike Yaconelli told about a girl in his youth group. One day he preached about God's love, and afterwards this sixteen-year-old girl comes up to him and says, "I've got this idea. When the carnival comes and all the carnies come in, wouldn't it be cool if we threw them a party to welcome them to town?"

BRENDA: At that time they always made fun of those people. They'd say, "Lock your doors. The carnival's coming to town." So, to show God's love, she thought it would be a good idea to welcome them and make them feel loved.

RICK: Mike said, "That's a good idea. We'll do that next year." A year goes by and the fair is coming to town. And the girl says, "Mike, remember the idea about the party for the carnies?" He says, "Oh, yeah. Okay, let's do it." So they call a meeting of the church and tell them the idea. But who's going to head up the party? When no one raises their hand, the girl volunteers. She calls the manager of the carnival, gives them the invitation, finds out how many people there are, and so forth.

The night of the party the carnies are late, and everyone's wondering if they're going to come. Well, they showed up—all two hundred of them. And they had this great party. The carnies were touched; this was a first for them. They took up an offering and got five hundred dollars, which they gave to the youth group. So next year they are planning to do a steak and lobster dinner! Isn't that wonderful?

When I heard that story, I wept. I think it describes where the heart of God is. Working with the street people for me was a similar kind of thing. I didn't want to do it at first, but the Lord sent me, and He opened my eyes to what those people are about and where their need is. You not only give to them; they give back to you.

Here's another story. We free-lance; that's our livelihood. About six months ago we hit the bottom, and Brenda panicked. At the same time, in our small group at church we were studying this scripture from Jeremiah (29:11-14): " 'For I know the plans I have for you,' declares the Lord, 'plans to prosper you and not to harm you, plans to give you hope and a future. Then you will call upon me and come and pray to me, and I will listen to you. You will seek me and find me when you seek me with all your heart. I will be found by you,' declares the Lord."

Some of the myths about artists are that they are always broke, they don't become famous till they die, and they're loners. God began to tell us those myths weren't true—not for His people—and He began to dismantle them, one by one.

BRENDA: During this time that we were struggling financially, I kept a prayer journal. I wrote, "Help us, Lord; give us faith. We're broke again, with student loans to pay. I have a doctor's appointment today and I think I'm going to cancel. Lord, I'm drowning in worries and cares. Lord, what about your promises?" Then I started reading the Bible and writing down all the verses where it says that God will provide. A couple days later I said, "Lord, thank you. We still don't have any money, but I have some hope and trust in you. Forgive me for worrying. Lord, I love you. I know my suffering is nothing compared to Christ's. Lord, take away the anger in my heart when we have no money." Then I quoted the verse from Psalm 118 that says, "Save us, we beseech thee, oh Lord. Oh Lord, we beseech thee, give us success." And then I thanked the Lord for providing for us. He always kept us in food.

We talked to some friends of ours who have a similar problem with money, and they gave us a tape series called *Breaking the Spirit of Poverty.* One of the things this tape said to do to break the spirit of poverty was to give hilariously. We decided we'd do that. We didn't have money, so we thought, Well, what can we give? Finally, I decided to use some ingredients I had in the cupboard and make cookies for the neighbors. It was embarrassing, since I didn't know them very well, but I did. Then Rick decided to give a print away to some friends of ours, a struggling young family who had admired some of his work.

There was an almost intoxicating feeling when we did this. We just felt silly, and a lot of the oppression we were feeling about not being able to pay the bills just lifted. We trusted God so much that He would honor us and honor His promises that we felt safe in the midst of all this reality.

One of the things that kept getting us into debt was our car. It was nice-looking, but everything on it kept going wrong. So we decided to sell it and live without a car.

RICK: Grand Rapids isn't like Chicago, by the way. It's a little harder to get around without a car.

BRENDA: After advertising in the paper and with a sign, we finally sold the car, and that helped pay some of the bills.

RICK: As soon as we'd decided we'd go without a car, some people who didn't know about our decision gave us a car! A couple days later, somebody else gave us a car. They were crummy cars, but they were cars. One worked for two weeks, and one got us to Cornerstone Festival. Isn't that wild? I felt like God had taken us up on His shoulders just like a father with his child.

BRENDA: Another myth that God exploded for us was the myth that artists are loners. As Christians, it's important for us to be integrated in a body of Christ. We need people to share with and pray with. Rick and I came to a point in our lives when we decided it wasn't good for us to be alone anymore. So we really started getting involved in church. Now, as an artist you tend to hang out with people who are like you. But in the church there are a lot of people who aren't like you. There are people who have jobs as truck drivers, accountants, or something, and they don't wear trendy clothes, dangly earrings, or whatever you're into. Many artists are snobs, in a way; they just want to hang out with people like themselves. What's really important, though, is that you all love the Lord. Being a part of a body has made a difference in our lives. The Lord has called us again and again in our weakness to reach out to people.

For a while, Rick and I were really into wearing a "Big Man's Hat," as Charlie Peacock's song puts it. We struggled with pride and thought we could do it all on our own. But the Lord says, "No, you can't do anything without me."

RICK: I used to be very self-confident, but God's not interested in that. I am not into being weak, but He is. So I've been boasting about my weakness a lot—maybe too much—because it's a new discovery for me. But that feeling of weakness is okay. God brings those He loves—like David and Jesus—to the wilderness. The wilderness really *is* your friend.

*We pray that the Lord would open your eyes to see what it is that keeps you from walking fully with Him. He loves you, and for your own good He will weed out your garden and prune your branches. It hurts, but in the long run you will produce fruit that will last and glorify God, whom you serve. May you fulfill the purpose for which you were created. In Jesus' name, Amen* (John 15:1-2)

# ENDNOTES

## CHAPTER 2

### *Like a House on Fire*

1. D. Johnson Fleming, *Each with His Own Brush: Contemporary Christian Art in Asia and Africa* (New York: Friendship Press, 1938).
2. Thomas M. Davis, "The Traditions of Puritan Typology," in *Typology and Early American Literature*, ed. Sacvan Bercovitch (Amherst, Mass.: University of Massachusetts Press, 1972), 32.

## CHAPTER 3

### *Abstract Art and Spirituality*

1. Hans Hofmann, *Search for the Real*, eds. Sara T. Weeks and Bartlett H. Hayes, Jr.(Cambridge, Mass.: The M.I.T. Press, 1967), 72.
2. Rupert Martin, "The Icon," in *New Icons: Christian Iconography in Contemporary Art* (Warwick, England: The University of Warwick, 1989).
3. Thomas Traherne, *Selected Poems and Prose* (London: Penguin Books, 1991), 224.
4. Thomas Merton, "Sacred Art and the Spiritual Life," in *Disputed Questions*, ed. Thomas P. McDowell (London: Hollis and Carter, 1960), 154.
5. Ibid., 155–156.
6. Ibid., 156.

### *Raids on the Inarticulate*

1. W. S. Graham, *Collected Poems 1942*–1947 (London: Faber and Faber, 1979), 155.
2. Dorothy Sayers, *The Mind of the Maker* (London: Methuen, 1941), 150.
3. John Wilson, *One of the Richest Gifts* (Edinburgh: The Handsel Press, 1981), 76.
4. Ibid., 77.
5. John Calvin, *Institutes of the Christian Religion*, bk. 2, ch. 2, sec. 15.
6. Louis MacNeice, *Snow*, in *Selected Poems of Louis MacNeice*, ed. W. H. Auden (London: Faber and Faber, 1964), 26.
7. T. S. Eliot, *The Four Quartets*, in *Collected Poems 1909*–1962 (London: Faber and Faber, 1963), 202–203.
8. Ibid., 203.
9. Rupert M. Loydell, *Quartet*, in *Fill These Days: New and Selected Poems* (Exeter, England: Stride, 1990), 41–70.
10. Wilson, *Richest Gifts*, 79.

# SUGGESTED READING

For more information on the Arts and Christian life, we suggest that you contact one of the following organizations/publications.

*Cornerstone* Magazine
939 West Wilson Avenue, Dept. BB
Chicago, IL 60640

YWAM (Colin Harbinson)
P.O. Box 1324
Cambridge, Ontario
Canada
N1R 7G6

Stride Publishing (Rupert Loydell)
37 Portland Street
Exeter
Devon EX1 2EG
England

Christians in the Arts Networking, Inc. (CAN)
9 Court St., 2nd Floor
P.O. Box 242
Arlington, MA 02174-0003

Christians in the Visual Arts (CIVA Newsletter)
P.O. Box 10247
Arlington, VA 22210